THE ALCHEMY OF HAPPINESS

D1881343

WISDOM OF THE EAST

THE ALCHEMY OF HAPPINESS

By

AL GHAZZALI

TRANSLATED FROM THE HINDUSTANI

BY CLAUD FIELD

GYAN

Published by

Gyan Publishing House
5, Ansari Road
Daryaganj, New Delhi-110002
Phone: 011-47034999, 9811692060
E-mail: books@gyanbooks.com

Distribution Network
gyanbooks.com
India, USA, Canada, UK, Australia, France

© Publisher

All rights reserved. No part of this work may be reproduced, stored, adapted, or transmitted in any form or by any means, electronic, mechanical, photocopying, micro-filming, recording or otherwise, or translated in any language, without the prior written permission of the copyright owner and the publisher.

ISBN: 978-81-212-6872-1 (PB)
First Published, 1910

2nd Impression 2023

Printed at: Gyan Press, Delhi.

The book is sold subject to the condition that it shall not, by way of trade or otherwise, be lent, resold, hired out, or otherwise circulated without the prior publisher's written consent.

THE ALCHEMY OF HAPPINESS
Author: AL GHAZZALI

WISDOM OF THE EAST

THE ALCHEMY OF HAPPINESS

BY AL GHAZZALI

TRANSLATED FROM THE HINDUSTANI
BY CLAUD FIELD

"Knowledge of a part is better than ignorance of the whole" (Abu'l Feda)

1910

CONTENTS

EDITORIAL NOTE

THE object of the Editors of this series is a very definite one. They desire above all things that, in their humble way, these books shall be the ambassadors of good-will and understanding between East and West—the old world of Thought and the new of Action. In this endeavour, and in their own sphere, they are but followers of the highest example in the land. They are confident that a deeper knowledge of the great ideals and lofty philosophy of Oriental thought may help to a revival of that true spirit of Charity which neither despises nor fears the nations of another creed and colour. Finally, in thanking press and public for the very cordial reception given to the "Wisdom of the East" Series, they wish to state that no pains have been spared to secure the best specialists for the treatment of the various subjects at hand.

L. CRANMER-BYNG.
S. A. KAPADIA.

NORTHBROOK SOCIETY,
185 PICCADILLY, W.

PREFACE

Renan, whose easy-going mind was the exact antithesis to the intense earnestness of Ghazzali, calls him "the most original mind among Arabian philosophers." [1] Notwithstanding this, his fame as a philosopher has been greatly overshadowed by Avicenna, his predecessor, and Averroes, his successor and opponent. It is a significant fact that the *Encyclopædia Britannica* devotes five columns to each of the others and only a column and a half to Ghazzali. Yet it is doubtful whether it is as a philosopher that he would have wished to be chiefly remembered. Several of his works, it is true, are polemics against the philosophers, especially his *Tehafot-al-falasifa*, or "Destruction of the Philosophers," and, as Solomon Munk says in his *Mélanges de philosophie Juive et Arabe*, Ghazzali dealt "a fatal blow" to Arabian philosophy in the East, from which it never recovered, though it revived for a while in Spain and culminated in Averroes. Philosopher and sceptic as he was by nature, Ghazzali's chief work was that of a theologian, moralist, and

[1] Renan: *Averroes et Averroisme.*

mystic, though his mysticism was strongly balanced by common sense. He had, as he tells us in his *Confessions*, experienced "conversion"; God had arrested him "on the edge of the fire," and thenceforth what Browning says of the French poet, René Gentilhomme, was true of him:

> Human praises scare
> Rather than soothe ears all a-tingle yet
> With tones few hear and live, and none forget.

In the same work he tells us that one of his besetting weaknesses had been the craving for applause, and in his *Ihya ul-ulum* ("Revival of the Religious Sciences") he devotes a long chapter to the dangers involved in a love of notoriety and the cure for it.

After his conversion he retired into religious seclusion for eleven years at Damascus (a corner of the mosque there still bears his name—"The Ghazzali Corner") and Jerusalem, where he gave himself up to intense and prolonged meditation. But he was too noble a character to concentrate himself entirely on his own soul and its eternal prospects. The requests of his children—and other family affairs of which we have no exact information—caused him to return home. Besides this, the continued progress of the Ismailians (connected with the famous Assassins), the spread of irreligious doctrines and the increasing religious indifference of the masses not only filled Ghazzali and his Sufi friends with profound grief, but determined them to stem the evil with the whole force of their philosophy, the ardour of vital conviction, and the authority of noble example.

In his autobiography referred to above Ghazzali tells us that, after emerging from a state of Pyrrhonic scepticism, he had finally arrived at the conclusion that the mystics were on the right path and true "Arifin," or Knowers of God.[1] But in saying this he meant those Sufis whose mysticism did not carry them into extravagant utterances like that of Mansur Hallaj, who was crucified at Bagdad (A.D. 922) for exclaiming "I am the Truth, or God." In his *Ihya-ul-ulum* Ghazzali says: "The matter went so far that certain persons boasted of a union with the Deity, and that in His unveiled presence they beheld Him, and enjoyed familiar converse with Him, saying, 'Thus it was spoken unto us and thus we speak.' Bayazid Bistami (*ob.* A.D. 875) is reported to have exclaimed, 'Glory be to me!' This style of discourse exerts a very pernicious influence on the common people. Some husbandmen indeed, letting their farms run to waste, set up similar pretensions for themselves; for human nature is pleased with maxims like these,

[1] It may be noted that there was a contemporary sect called "La-adria"—agnostics.

which permit one to neglect useful labour with the idea of acquiring spiritual purity through the attainment of certain mysterious degrees and qualities. This notion is productive of great injury, so that the death of one of these foolish babblers would be a greater benefit to the cause of true religion than the saving alive of ten of them."

For himself Ghazzali was a practical mystic. His aim was to make men better by leading them from a merely notional acquiescence in the stereotyped creed of Islam to a real knowledge of God. The first four chapters of *The Alchemy of Happiness* are a commentary on the famous verse in the *Hadis* (traditional sayings of Muhammad), "He who knows himself knows God." He is especially scornful of the parrot-like repetition of orthodox phrases. Thus alluding to the almost hourly use by Muhammadans of the phrase, "I take refuge in God" (*Ma'udhib'illah!*), Ghazzali says, in the *Ihya-ul-ulum*: "Satan laughs at such pious ejaculations. Those who utter them are like a man who should meet a lion in a desert, while there is a fort at no great distance, and, when he sees the evil beast, should stand exclaiming, 'I take refuge in that fortress,' without moving a step towards it. What will such an ejaculation profit him? In the same way the mere exclamation, 'I take refuge in God,' will not protect thee from the terrors of His judgment unless thou really take refuge in Him." It is related of some unknown Sufi that when asked for a definition of religious sincerity he drew a red-hot piece of iron out of a blacksmith's forge, and said, "Behold it!" This "red-hot" sincerity is certainly characteristic of Ghazzali, and there is no wonder that he did not admire his contemporary, Omar Khayyám.

The little picture of the lion and the fort in the above passage is a small instance of another conspicuous trait in Ghazzali's mind—his turn for allegory. Emerson says, "Whoever thinks intently will find an image more or less luminous rise in his mind." In Ghazzali's writings many such images arise, some grotesque and some beautiful. His allegory of the soul as a fortress beleaguered by the "armies of Satan" is a striking anticipation of the *Holy War* of Bunyan. The greatest of all the Sufi poets, Jalaluddin Rumi, born a century after Ghazzali's death (A.D. 1207), has paid him the compliment of incorporating several of these allegories which occur in the *Ihya* into his own *Masnavi*. Such is the famous one of the Chinese and Greek artists, which runs as follows:

"Once upon a time the Chinese having challenged the Greeks to a trial of skill in painting, the Sultan summoned them both into edifices built for the purpose directly facing each other, and commanded them to show proof of their art.

The painters of the two nations immediately applied themselves with diligence to their work. The Chinese sought and obtained of the king every day a great quantity of colours, but the Greeks not the least particle. Both worked in profound silence, until the Chinese, with a clangor of cymbals and of trumpets, announced the end of their labours. Immediately the king, with his courtiers, hastened to their temple, and there stood amazed at the wonderful splendour of the Chinese painting and the exquisite beauty of the colours. But meanwhile the Greeks, who had not sought to adorn the walls with paints, but laboured rather to erase every colour, drew aside the veil which concealed their work. Then, wonderful to tell, the manifold variety of the Chinese colours was seen still more delicately and beautifully reflected from the walls of the Grecian temple, as it stood illuminated by the rays of the midday sun."

This parable, of course, illustrates the favourite Sufi tenet that the heart must be kept pure and calm as an unspotted mirror. Similarly, the apologue of the elephant in the dark (*vide* chap. II.) has been borrowed by Jalaluddin Rumi from Ghazzali.

Another characteristic of Ghazzali which appeals to the modern mind is the way in which he expounds the religious argument from probability much as Bishop Butler and Browning do (*vide* the end of Chapter IV. in the present book). Ghazzali might have said, with Blougram:

> With me faith means perpetual unbelief
> Kept quiet like the snake 'neath Michael's foot,
> Who stands calm just because he feels it writhe.

This combination of ecstatic assurance and scepticism is one of those antinomies of the human mind which annoy the rationalist and rejoice the mystic. Those in whom they co-exist, like Ghazzali in the eleventh century and Cardinal Newman in the nineteenth, are a perpetual problem to understand and therefore perennially interesting:

> He may believe, and yet, and yet,
> How can he?

Another point in which Ghazzali anticipates Bishop Butler is his representation of punishment as the natural working out of consequences, and not an arbitrary infliction imposed *ab extra*. He tries to rationalise the lurid threatenings of the Koran.

In his own day Ghazzali was accused of having one doctrine for the multitude and one for himself and his intimate friends. Professor D. B. Macdonald, of Hartford, after going thoroughly into the matter, says, "If the charge of a secret doctrine is to be proved against Ghazzali it must be on other and better evidence than that which is now before us."

At any rate, Ghazzali has been accepted as an orthodox authority by the Muhammadans, among whom his title is Hujjat-el-Islam, "The Proof of Islam," and it has been said, "If all the books of Islam were destroyed it would be but a slight loss if only the *Ihya* of Ghazzali were preserved." The great modern reformer of Islam in India, the late Sir Syud Ahmed, has had some portions of this enormous work printed separately for the purpose of familiarising the young Moslems at Aligarh with Ghazzali.

The *Ihya* was written in Arabic, and Ghazzali himself wrote an abridgment of it in Persian for popular use which he entitled *Kimiya'e Saadat* ("The Alchemy of Happiness"). This little book contains eight sections of that abridgment.

Theologians are the best judges of theologians, and in conclusion we may quote Dr. August Tholuck's opinion of Ghazzali: "This man, if ever any have deserved the name, was truly a 'divine,' and he may be justly placed on a level with Origen, so remarkable was he for learning and ingenuity, and gifted with such a rare faculty for the skilful and worthy exposition of doctrine. All that is good, noble, and sublime that his great soul had compassed he bestowed upon Muhammadanism, and he adorned the doctrines of the Koran with so much piety and learning that, in the form given them by him, they seem, in my opinion, worthy the assent of Christians. Whatsoever was most excellent in the philosophy of Aristotle or in the Sufic mysticism he discreetly adapted to the Muhammadan theology; from every school he sought the means of shedding light and honour upon religion; while his sincere piety and lofty conscientiousness imparted to all his writings a sacred majesty. He was the first of Muhammadan divines."

THE ALCHEMY OF HAPPINESS

INTRODUCTION

KNOW, O beloved, that man was not created in jest or at random, but marvellously made and for some great end. Although he is not from everlasting, yet he lives for ever; and though his body is mean and earthly, yet his spirit is lofty and divine. When in the crucible of abstinence he is purged from carnal passions he attains to the highest, and in place of being a slave to lust and anger becomes endued with angelic qualities. Attaining that state, he finds his heaven in the contemplation of Eternal Beauty, and no longer in fleshly delights. The spiritual alchemy which operates this change in him, like that which transmutes base metals into gold, is not easily discovered, nor to be found in the house of every old woman. It is to explain that alchemy and its methods of operation that the author has undertaken this work, which he has entitled, *The Alchemy of Happiness*. Now the treasuries of God, in which this alchemy is to be sought, are the hearts of the prophets, and he who seeks it elsewhere will be disappointed and bankrupt on the day of judgment when he hears the words, "We have lifted the veil from off thee, and thy sight to-day is keen."

God has sent on earth a hundred and twenty-four thousand prophets[1] to teach men the prescription of this alchemy, and how to purify their hearts from baser qualities in the crucible of abstinence. This alchemy may be briefly described as turning away from the world to God, and its constituents are four:

1. The knowledge of self.
2. The knowledge of God.
3. The knowledge of this world as it really is.
4. The knowledge of the next world as it really is.

We shall now proceed to expound these four constituents in order.

[1] This is the fixed number of the prophets according to Muhammadan tradition.

CHAPTER I

THE KNOWLEDGE OF SELF

KNOWLEDGE of self is the key to the knowledge of God, according to the saying: "He who knows himself knows God,"[1] and, as it is written in the Koran, "We will show them Our signs in the world and *in themselves*, that the truth may be manifest to them." Now nothing is nearer to thee than thyself, and if thou knowest not thyself how canst thou know anything else? If thou sayest "I know myself," meaning thy outward shape, body, face, limbs, and so forth, such knowledge can never be a key to the knowledge of God. Nor, if thy knowledge as to that which is within only extends so far, that when thou art hungry thou eatest, and when thou art angry thou attackest some one, wilt thou progress any further in this path, for the beasts are thy partners in this. But real self-knowledge consists in knowing the following things: What art thou in thyself, and from whence hast thou come? Whither

[1] Traditional saying of Muhammad.

art thou going, and for what purpose hast thou come to tarry here awhile, and in what does thy real happiness and misery consist? Some of thy attributes are those of animals, some of devils, and some of angels, and thou hast to find out which of these attributes are accidental and which essential. Till thou knowest this, thou canst not find out where thy real happiness lies. The occupation of animals is eating, sleeping, and fighting; therefore, if thou art an animal, busy thyself in these things. Devils are busy in stirring up mischief, and in guile and deceit; if thou belongest to them, do their work. Angels contemplate the beauty of God, and are entirely free from animal qualities; if thou art of angelic nature, then strive towards thine origin, that thou mayest know and contemplate the Most High, and be delivered from the thraldom of lust and anger. Thou shouldest also discover why thou hast been created with these two animal instincts: whether that they should subdue and lead thee captive, or whether that thou shouldest subdue them, and, in thy upward progress, make of one thy steed and of the other thy weapon.

The first step to self-knowledge is to know that thou art composed of an outward shape, called the body, and an inward entity called the heart, or soul. By "heart," I do not mean the piece of flesh situated in the left of our bodies, but that which uses all the other faculties as its instruments and servants. In truth it does not belong to the visible world, but to the invisible, and has come into this world as a traveller visits a foreign country for the sake of merchandise, and will presently return to its native land. It is the knowledge of this entity and its attributes which is the key to the knowledge of God.

Some idea of the reality of the heart, or spirit, may be obtained by a man closing his eyes and forgetting everything around except his individuality. He will thus also obtain a glimpse of the unending nature of that individuality. Too close inquiry, however, into the essence of spirit is forbidden by the Law. In the Koran it is written: "They will question thee concerning the spirit. Say: 'The Spirit comes by the command of my Lord.'" Thus much is known of it that it is an indivisible essence belonging to the world of decrees, and that it is not from everlasting, but created. An exact philosophical knowledge of the spirit is not a necessary preliminary to walking in the path of religion, but comes rather as the result of self-discipline and perseverance in that path, as it is said in the Koran: "Those who strive in our way, verily we will guide them to the right paths."

For the carrying on of this spiritual warfare by which the knowledge of oneself and of God is to be obtained, the body may be figured as a kingdom, the soul as its king, and the different senses and faculties as constituting an army. Reason may be called the vizier, or prime minister, passion the revenue-collector, and anger the police-officer. Under the guise of collecting revenue, passion is continually prone to plunder on its own account, while resentment is always inclined to harshness and extreme severity. Both of these, the revenue-collector and the police-officer, have to be kept in due subordination to the king, but not killed or expelled, as they have their own proper functions to fulfil. But if passion and resentment master reason, the ruin of the soul infallibly ensues. A soul which allows its lower faculties to dominate the higher is as one who should hand over an angel to the power of a dog or a Mussalman to the tyranny of an unbeliever. The cultivation of demonic, animal, or angelic qualities results in the production of corresponding characters, which in the Day of Judgment will be manifested in visible shapes, the sensual appearing as swine, the ferocious as dogs and wolves, and the pure as angels. The aim of moral discipline is to purify the heart from the rust of passion and resentment, till, like a clear mirror, it reflects the light of God.

Some one may here object, "But if man has been created with animal and demonic qualities as well as angelic, how are we to know that the latter constitute his real essence, while the former are merely accidental and transitory?" To this I answer that the essence of each creature is to be sought in that which is highest in it and peculiar to it. Thus the horse and the ass are both burden-bearing animals, but the superiority of the horse to the ass consists in its being adapted for use in battle. If it fails in this, it becomes degraded to the rank of burden-bearing animals. Similarly with man: the highest faculty in him is reason, which fits him for the contemplation of God. If this predominates in him, when he dies, he leaves behind him all tendencies to passion and resentment, and becomes capable of association with angels. As regards his mere animal qualities, man is inferior to many animals, but reason makes him superior to them, as it is written in the Koran: "To man we have subjected all things in the earth." But if his lower tendencies have triumphed, after death he will ever be looking towards the earth and longing for earthly delights.

Now the rational soul in man abounds in marvels, both of knowledge and power. By means of it he masters arts and sciences, can pass in a flash from earth to heaven and back again, can map out the skies and measure the distances between the stars. By it also he can draw the fish from the sea and the birds from the air, and can subdue to his service animals like the elephant, the camel, and the horse. His five senses are like five doors opening on the external world; but, more wonderful than this, his heart has a window which opens on the unseen world of spirits. In the state of sleep, when the avenues of the senses are closed, this window is opened and man receives impressions from the unseen world and sometimes foreshadowings of the future. His heart is then like a mirror which reflects what is pictured in the Tablet of Fate. But, even in sleep, thoughts of worldly things dull this mirror, so that the impressions it receives are not clear. After death, however, such thoughts vanish and things are seen in their naked reality, and the saying in the Koran is fulfilled: "We have stripped the veil from off thee and thy sight to-day is keen."

This opening of a window in the heart towards the unseen also takes place in conditions approaching those of prophetic inspiration, when intuitions spring up in the mind unconveyed through any sense-channel. The more a man purifies himself from fleshly lusts and concentrates his mind on God, the more conscious will he be of such intuitions. Those who are not conscious of them have no right to deny their reality.

Nor are such intuitions confined only to those of prophetic rank. Just as iron, by sufficient polishing, can be made into a mirror, so any mind by due discipline can be rendered receptive of such impressions. It was at this truth the Prophet hinted when he said, "Every child is born with a predisposition towards Islam; then his parents make a Jew, or a Christian, or a star-worshipper of him." Every human being has in the depths of his consciousness heard the question "Am I not your Lord?" and answered "Yes" to it. But some hearts are like mirrors so befouled with rust and dirt that they give no clear reflections, while those of the prophets and saints, though they are men "of like passions with us," are extremely sensitive to all divine impressions.

Nor is it only by reason of knowledge acquired and intuitive that the soul of man holds the first rank among created things, but also by reason of power. Just as angels preside over the elements, so does the soul rule the members of the body. Those souls which attain a special degree of power not only rule their own body but those of others also. If they wish a sick man to recover he recovers, or a person in health to fall ill he becomes ill, or if they will the presence of a person he comes to them. According as the effects produced by these powerful souls are good or bad they are termed miracles or sorceries. These souls differ from common folk in three ways: (1) What others only see in dreams they see in their waking moments. (2) While others' wills only affect their own bodies, these, by will-power, can move bodies extraneous to themselves.

(3) The knowledge which others acquire by laborious learning comes to them by intuition.

These three, of course, are not the only marks which differentiate them from common people, but the only ones that come within our cognisance. Just as no one knows the real nature of God but God Himself, so no one knows the real nature of a prophet but a prophet. Nor is this to be wondered at, as in every-day matters we see that it is impossible to explain the charm of poetry to one whose ear is insusceptible of cadence and rhythm, or the glories of colour to one who is stone-blind. Besides mere incapacity, there are other hindrances to the attainment of spiritual truth. One of these is externally acquired knowledge. To use a figure, the heart may be represented as a well, and the five senses as five streams which are continually conveying water to it. In order to find out the real contents of the heart these streams must be stopped for a time, at any rate, and the refuse they have brought with them must be cleared out of the well. In other words, if we are to arrive at pure spiritual truth, we must put away, for the time, knowledge which has been acquired by external processes and which too often hardens into dogmatic prejudice.

A mistake of an opposite kind is made by shallow people who, echoing some phrases which they have caught from Sufi teachers, go about decrying all knowledge. This is as if a person who was not an adept in alchemy were to go about saying, "Alchemy is better than gold," and were to refuse gold when it was offered to him. Alchemy *is* better than gold, but real alchemists are very rare, and so are real Sufis. He who has a mere smattering of Sufism is not superior to a learned man, any more than he who has tried a few experiments in alchemy has ground for despising a rich man.

Any one who will look into the matter will see that happiness is necessarily linked with the knowledge of God. Each faculty of ours delights in that for which it was created: lust delights in accomplishing desire, anger in taking vengeance, the eye in seeing beautiful objects, and the ear in hearing harmonious sounds. The highest function of the soul of man is the perception of truth; in this accordingly it finds its special delight. Even in trifling matters, such as learning chess, this holds good, and the higher the subject-matter of the knowledge obtained the greater the delight. A man would be pleased at being admitted into the confidence of a prime minister, but how much more if the king makes an intimate of him and discloses state secrets to him!

An astronomer who, by his knowledge, can map the stars and describe their courses, derives more pleasure from his knowledge than the chess-player from his. Seeing, then, that nothing is higher than God, how great must be the delight which springs from the true knowledge of Him!

A person in whom the desire for this knowledge has disappeared is like one who has lost his appetite for healthy food, or who prefers feeding on clay to eating bread. All bodily appetites perish at death with the organs they use, but the soul dies not, and retains whatever knowledge of God it possesses; nay, increases it.

An important part of our knowledge of God arises from the study and contemplation of our own bodies, which reveal to us the power, wisdom, and love of the Creator. His power, in that from a mere drop He has built up the wonderful frame of man; His wisdom is revealed in its intricacies and the mutual adaptibility of its parts; and His love is shown by His not only supplying such organs as are absolutely necessary for existence, as the liver, the heart, and the brain, but those which are not absolutely necessary, as the hand, the foot, the tongue, and the eye. To these He has added, as ornaments, the blackness of the hair, the redness of lips, and the curve of the eyebrows.

Man has been truly termed a "microcosm," or little world in himself, and the structure of his body should be studied not only by those who wish to become doctors, but by those who wish to attain to a more intimate knowledge of God, just as close study of the niceties and shades of language in a great poem reveals to us more and more of the genius of its author.

But, when all is said, the knowledge of the soul plays a more important part in leading to the knowledge of God than the knowledge of our body and its functions. The body may be compared to a steed and the soul to its rider; the body was created for the soul, the soul for the body. If a man knows not his own soul, which is the nearest thing to him, what is the use of his claiming to know others? It is as if a beggar who has not the wherewithal for a meal should claim to be able to feed a town.

In this chapter we have attempted, in some degree, to expound the greatness of man's soul. He who neglects it and suffers its capacities to rust or to degenerate must necessarily be the loser in this world and the next. The true greatness of man lies in his capacity for eternal progress, otherwise in this temporal sphere he is the weakest of all things, being subject to hunger, thirst, heat, cold, and sorrow. Those things he takes most delight in are often the most injurious to him, and those things which benefit him are not to be obtained without toil and trouble. As to his intellect, a slight disarrangement of matter in his brain is sufficient to destroy or madden him; as to his power, the sting of a wasp is sufficient to rob him of ease and sleep; as to his temper, he is upset by the loss of a sixpence; as to his beauty, he is little more than nauseous matter covered with a fair skin. Without frequent washing he becomes utterly repulsive and disgraceful.

In truth, man in this world is extremely weak and contemptible; it is only in the next that he will be of value, if by means of the "alchemy of happiness" he rises from the rank of beasts to that of angels. Otherwise his condition will be worse than the brutes, which perish and turn to dust. It is necessary for him, at the same time that he is conscious of his superiority as the climax of created things, to learn to know also his helplessness, as that too is one of the keys to the knowledge of God.

CHAPTER II

THE KNOWLEDGE OF GOD

It is a well-known saying of the Prophet that "He who knows himself, knows God"; that is, by contemplation of his own being and attributes man arrives at some knowledge of God. But since many who contemplate themselves do not find God, it follows that there must be some special way of doing so. As a matter of fact, there are two methods of arriving at this knowledge, but one is so abstruse that it is not adapted to ordinary intelligences, and therefore is better left unexplained. The other method is as follows: When a man considers himself he knows that there was a time when he was non-existent, as it is written in the Koran: "Does it not occur to man that there was a time when he was nothing?" Further, he knows that he was made out of a drop of water in which there was neither intellect, nor hearing, sight, head, hands, feet, etc. From this it is obvious that, whatever degree of perfection he may have arrived at, he did not make himself, nor can he now make a single hair.

How much more helpless, then, was his condition when he was a mere drop of water! Thus, as we have seen in the first chapter, he finds in his own being reflected in miniature, so to speak, the power, wisdom, and love of the Creator. If all the sages of the world were assembled, and their lives prolonged for an indefinite time, they could not effect any improvement in the construction of a single part of the body.

For instance, in the adaptation of the front and side-teeth to the mastication of food, and in the construction of the tongue, salivating glands, and throat for its deglutition, we find a contrivance which cannot be improved upon. Similarly, whoever considers his hand, with its five fingers of unequal lengths, four of them with three joints and the thumb with only two, and the way in which it can be used for grasping, or for carrying, or for smiting, will frankly acknowledge that no amount of human wisdom could better it by altering the number and arrangement of the fingers, or in any other way.

When a man further considers how his various wants of food, lodging, etc., are amply supplied from the storehouse of creation, he becomes aware that God's mercy is as great as His power and wisdom, as He has Himself said, "My mercy is greater than My wrath," and according to the Prophet's saying, "God is more tender to His servants than a mother to her suckling-child."

Thus from his own creation man comes to know God's existence, from the wonders of his bodily frame God's power and wisdom, and from the ample provision made for his various needs God's love. In this way the knowledge of oneself becomes a key to the knowledge of God.

Not only are man's attributes a reflection of God's attributes, but the mode of existence of man's soul affords some insight into God's mode of existence. That is to say, both God and the soul are invisible, indivisible, unconfined by space and time, and outside the categories of quantity and quality; nor can the ideas of shape, colour, or size attach to them. People find it hard to form a conception of such realities as are devoid of quality and quantity, etc., but a similar difficulty attaches to the conception of our everyday feelings, such as anger, pain, pleasure, or love. They are thought-concepts, and cannot be cognised by the senses; whereas quality, quantity, etc., are sense-concepts. Just as the ear cannot take cognisance of colour, nor the eye of sound, so, in conceiving of the ultimate realities, God and the soul, we find ourselves in a region in which sense-concepts can bear no part. So much, however, we can see, that, as God is Ruler of the universe, and, being Himself beyond space and time, quantity and quality, governs things that are so conditioned, so the soul rules the body and its members, being itself invisible, indivisible, and unlocated in any special part. For how can the indivisible be located in that which is divisible? From all this we see how true is the saying of the Prophet, "God created man in His own likeness."

And, as we arrive at some knowledge of God's essence and attributes from the contemplation of the soul's essence and attributes, so we come to understand God's method of working and government and delegation of power to angelic forces, etc., by observing how each of us governs his own little kingdom. To take a simple instance: suppose a man wishes to write the name of God. First of all the wish is conceived in his heart, it is then conveyed to the brain by the vital spirits, the form of the word "God" takes shape in the thought-chambers of the brain, thence it travels by the nerve-channels, and sets in motion the fingers, which in their turn set in motion the pen, and thus the name "God" is traced on paper exactly as it had been conceived in the writer's brain. Similarly, when God wills a thing it appears in the spiritual plane, which in the Koran is called "The Throne"[1]; from the throne it passes, by a spiritual current, to a lower plane called "The Chair"[2]; then the shape of it appears on the "Tablet of Destiny"[3]; whence, by the mediation of the forces called "angels," it assumes actuality, and appears on the earth in the form of plants, trees, and animals, repre-

[1] Al Arsh. [2] Al Kursi. [3] Al Lauh Al Mahfuz.

senting the will and thought of God, as the written letters represent the wish conceived in the heart and the shape present in the brain of the writer.

No one can understand a king but a king; therefore God has made each of us a king in miniature, so to speak, over a kingdom which is an infinitely reduced copy of His own. In the kingdom of man God's "throne" is represented by the soul, the Archangel by the heart, "the chair" by the brain, "the tablet" by the treasure-chamber of thought. The soul, itself unlocated and indivisible, governs the body as God governs the universe. In short, each of us is entrusted with a little kingdom, and charged not to be careless in the administration of it.

As regards the recognition of God's providence, there are many degrees of knowledge. The mere physicist is like an ant who, crawling on a sheet of paper and observing black letters spreading over it, should refer the cause to the pen alone. The astronomer is like an ant of somewhat wider vision who should catch sight of the fingers moving the pen, *i.e.* he knows that the elements are under the power of the stars, but he does not know that the stars are under the power of the angels. Thus, owing to the different degrees of perception in people, disputes must arise in tracing effects to causes. Those whose eyes never see beyond the world of phenomena are like those who mistake servants of the lowest rank for the king. The laws of phenomena must be constant, or there could be no such thing as science; but it is a great error to mistake the slaves for the master.

As long as this difference in the perceptive faculty of observers exists, disputes must necessarily go on. It is as if some blind men, hearing that an elephant had come to their town, should go and examine it. The only knowledge of it which they can obtain comes through the sense of touch: so one handles the animal's leg, another his tusk, another his ear, and, according to their several perceptions, pronounce it to be a column, a thick pole, or a quilt, each taking a part for the whole. So the physicist and astronomer confound the laws they perceive with the Lawgiver. A similar mistake is attributed to Abraham in the Koran, where it is related that he turned successively to stars, moon, and sun as the objects of his worship, till, grown aware of Him who made all these, he exclaimed, "I love not them that set."

We have a common instance of this referring to second causes what ought to be referred to the First Cause in the case of so-called illness. For instance, if a man ceases to take any interest in worldly matters, conceives a distaste for common pleasures, and appears sunk in depression, the doctor will say, "This is a case of melancholy,

[1] Koran, chap. vi.

and requires such and such a prescription." The physicist will say, "This is a dryness of the brain caused by hot weather and cannot be relieved till the air becomes moist." The astrologer will attribute it to some particular conjunction or opposition of planets. "Thus far their wisdom reaches," says the Koran. It does not occur to them that what has really happened is this: that the Almighty has a concern for the welfare of that man, and has therefore commanded his servants, the planets or the elements, to produce such a condition in him that he may turn away from the world to his Maker. The knowledge of this fact is a lustrous pearl from the ocean of inspirational knowledge, to which all other forms of knowledge are as islands in the sea.

The doctor, physicist, and astrologer are doubtless right each in his particular branch of knowledge, but they do not see that illness is, so to speak, a cord of love by which God draws to Himself the saints concerning whom He has said, "I was sick and ye visited Me not." Illness itself is one of those forms of experience by which man arrives at the knowledge of God, as He says by the mouth of His Prophet, "Sicknesses themselves are My servants, and are attached to My chosen."

The foregoing remarks may enable us to enter a little more fully into the meaning of those exclamations so often on the lips of the Faithful: "God is holy," "Praise be to God," "There is no God but God," "God is great." Concerning the last we may say that it does not mean that God is greater than creation, for creation is His manifestation as light manifests the sun, and it would not be correct to say that the sun is greater than its own light. It rather means that God's greatness immeasurably transcends our cognitive faculties, and that we can only form a very dim and imperfect idea of it. If a child asks us to explain to him the pleasure which exists in wielding sovereignty, we may say it is like the pleasure he feels in playing bat and ball, though in reality the two have nothing in common except that they both come under the category of pleasure. Thus, the exclamation "God is great" means that His greatness far exceeds all our powers of comprehension. Moreover, such imperfect knowledge of God as we can attain to is not a mere speculative knowledge, but must be accompanied by devotion and worship. When a man dies he has to do with God alone, and if we have to live with a person, our happiness entirely depends on the degree of affection we feel towards him. Love is the seed of happiness, and love to God is fostered and developed by worship. Such worship and constant remembrance of God implies a certain degree of austerity and curbing of bodily appetites. Not that a man is intended altogether to abolish these, for then the human race would perish. But strict limits must be set to their indulgence, and as a man is not the best judge in his own case as to what these limits should be, he had better consult some spiritual guide on the subject. Such spiritual guides are the prophets, and the laws which they have laid down under divine inspiration prescribe the limits which must be observed in these matters. He who transgresses these limits "wrongs his own soul," as it is written in the Koran.

Notwithstanding this clear pronouncement of the Koran there are those who, through their ignorance of God, do transgress these limits, and this ignorance may be due to several different causes: Firstly, there are some who, failing to find God by observation, conclude that there is no God and that this world of wonders made itself, or existed from everlasting. They are like a man who, seeing a beautifully-written letter, should suppose that it had written itself without a writer, or had always existed. People in this state of mind are so far gone in error that it is of little use to argue with them. Such are some of the physicists and astronomers to whom we referred above.

Some, through ignorance of the real nature of the soul, repudiate the doctrine of a future life, in which man will be called to account and be rewarded or punished. They regard themselves as no better than animals or vegetables, and equally perishable. Some, on the other hand, believe in God and a future life, but with a weak belief. They say to themselves, "God is great and independent of us; our worship or abstinence from worship is a matter of entire indifference to Him." Their state of mind is like that of a sick man who, when prescribed a certain regime by his doctor, should say, "Well, if I follow it or don't follow it, what does it matter to the doctor?" It certainly does not matter to the doctor, but the patient may destroy himself by his disobedience. Just as surely as unchecked sickness of body ends in bodily death, so does uncured disease of the soul end in future misery, according to the saying of the Koran, "Only those shall be saved who come to God with a sound heart."

A fourth kind of unbelievers are those who say, "The Law tells us to abstain from anger, lust, and hypocrisy. This is plainly impossible, for man is created with these qualities inherent in him. You might as well tell us to make black white." These foolish people ignore the fact that the law does not tell us to uproot these passions, but to restrain them within due limits, so that, by avoiding the greater sins, we may obtain forgiveness of the smaller ones. Even the Prophet of God said, "I am a man like you, and get angry like others"; and in the Koran it is written, "God loves those who swallow down their anger," not those who have no anger at all.

A fifth class lay stress on the beneficence of God, and ignore His justice, saying to themselves, "Well, whatever we do, God is merciful." They do not consider that, though God is merciful, thousands of human beings perish miserably in hunger and disease. They know that whosoever wishes for a livelihood, or for wealth, or learning, must not merely say, "God is merciful," but must exert himself. Although the Koran says, "Every living creature's support comes from God," it is also written, "Man obtains nothing except by striving." The fact is, such teaching is really from the devil, and such people only speak with their lips and not with their heart.

A sixth class claim to have reached such a degree of sanctity that sin cannot affect them. Yet, if you treat one of them with disrespect, he will bear a grudge against you for years, and if one of them be deprived of a morsel of food which he thinks his due, the whole world will appear dark and narrow to him. Even if any of them do really conquer their passions, they have no right to make such a claim, for the prophets, the highest of human kind, constantly confessed and bewailed their sins. Some of them had such a dread of sin that they even abstained from lawful things; thus, it is related of the Prophet that, one day, when a date had been brought to him he would not eat it, as he was not sure that it had been lawfully obtained. Whereas these free-livers will swallow gallons of wine and claim (I shudder as I write) to be superior to the Prophet whose sanctity was endangered by a date, while theirs is unaffected by all that wine! Surely they deserve that the devil should drag them down to perdition. Real saints know that he who does not master his appetites does not deserve the name of a man, and that the true Moslem is one who will cheerfully acknowledge the limits imposed by the Law. He who endeavours, on whatever pretext, to ignore its obligations is certainly under Satanic influence, and should be talked to, not with a pen, but with a sword. These pseudo-mystics sometimes pretend to be drowned in a sea of wonder, but if you ask them what they are wondering at they do not know. They should be told to wonder as much as they please, but at the same time to remember that the Almighty is their Creator and that they are His servants.

CHAPTER III

THE KNOWLEDGE OF THIS WORLD

THIS world is a stage or market-place passed by pilgrims on their way to the next. It is here that they are to provide themselves with provisions for the way; or, to put it plainly, man acquires here, by the use of his bodily senses, some knowledge of the works of God, and, through them, of God Himself, the sight of whom will constitute his future beatitude. It is for the acquirement of this knowledge that the spirit of man has descended into this world of water and clay. As long as his senses remain with him he is said to be "in this world"; when they depart, and only his essential attributes remain, he is said to have gone to "the next world."

While man is in this world, two things are necessary for him: first, the protection and nurture of his soul; secondly, the care and nurture of his body. The proper nourishment of the soul, as above shown, is the knowledge and love of God, and to be absorbed in the love of anything but

God is the ruin of the soul. The body, so to speak, is simply the riding-animal of the soul, and perishes while the soul endures. The soul should take care of the body, just as a pilgrim on his way to Mecca takes care of his camel; but if the pilgrim spends his whole time in feeding and adorning his camel, the caravan will leave him behind, and he will perish in the desert.

Man's bodily needs are simple, being comprised under three heads: food, clothing, and a dwelling-place; but the bodily desires which were implanted in him with a view to procuring these are apt to rebel against reason, which is of later growth than they. Accordingly, as we saw above, they require to be curbed and restrained by the divine laws promulgated by the prophets.

Considering the world with which we have for a time to do, we find it divided into three departments—animal, vegetable, and mineral. The products of all three are continually needed by man and have given rise to three principal occupations—those of the weaver, the builder, and the worker in metal. These, again, have many subordinate branches, such as tailors, masons, smiths, etc. None can be quite independent of others; this gives rise to various business-connections and relations, and these too frequently afford occasions for hatred, envy, jealousy, and other maladies of the soul. Hence come quarrels and strife, and the need of political and civil government and knowledge of law.

Thus the occupations and businesses of the world have become more and more complicated and troublesome, chiefly owing to the fact that men have forgotten that their real necessities are only three—clothing, food, and shelter, and that these exist only with the object of making the body a fit vehicle for the soul in its journey towards the next world. They have fallen into the same mistake as the pilgrim to Mecca, mentioned above, who, forgetting the object of his pilgrimage and himself, should spend his whole time in feeding and adorning his camel. Unless a man maintains the strictest watch he is certain to be fascinated and entangled by the world, which, as the Prophet said, is "a more potent sorcerer than Harut and Marut."[1]

The deceitful character of the world comes out in the following ways. In the first place, it pretends that it will always remain with you, while, as a matter of fact, it is slipping away from you, moment by moment, and bidding you farewell, like a shadow which seems stationary, but is actually always moving. Again, the world presents itself under the guise of a radiant but immoral sorceress, pretends to be in love with you, fondles you, and then goes off to your enemies, leaving you to die of chagrin and despair.

[1] Two fallen angels.

Jesus (upon whom be peace!) saw the world revealed in the form of an ugly old hag. He asked her how many husbands she had possessed; she replied that they were countless. He asked whether they had died or been divorced; she said that she had slain them all. "I marvel," he said, "at the fools who see what you have done to others, and still desire you."

This sorceress decks herself out in gorgeous and jewelled apparel and veils her face. Then she goes forth to seduce men, too many of whom follow her to their own destruction. The Prophet has said that in the Judgment Day the world will appear in the form of a hideous witch with green eyes and projecting teeth. Men, beholding her, will say, "Mercy on us! who is this?" The angels will answer, "This is the world for whose sake you quarrelled and fought and embittered one another's lives." Then she will be cast into hell, whence she will cry out, "O Lord! where are those, my former lovers?" God will then command that they be cast after her.

Whoever will seriously contemplate the past eternity during which the world was not in existence, and the future eternity during which it will not be in existence, will see that it is essentially like a journey, in which the stages are represented by years, the leagues by months, the miles by days, and the steps by moments. What words, then, can picture the folly of the man who endeavours to make it his permanent abode, and forms plans ten years ahead regarding things he may never need, seeing that very possibly he may be under the ground in ten days!

Those who have indulged without limit in the pleasures of the world, at the time of death will be like a man who has gorged himself to repletion on delicious viands and then vomits them up. The deliciousness has gone, but the disgrace remains. The greater the abundance of the possessions which they have enjoyed in the shape of gardens, male and female slaves, gold, silver, etc., the more keenly they will feel the bitterness of parting from them. This is a bitterness which will outlast death, for the soul which has contracted covetousness as a fixed habit will necessarily in the next world suffer from the pangs of unsatisfied desire.

Another dangerous property of worldly things is that they at first appear as mere trifles, but each of these so-called "trifles" branches out into countless ramifications until they swallow up the whole of a man's time and energy. Jesus (on whom be peace!) said, "The lover of the world is like a man drinking sea-water; the more he drinks, the more thirsty he gets, till at last he perishes with thirst unquenched." The Prophet said, "You can no more mix with the world without being contaminated by it than you can go into water without getting wet."

The world is like a table spread for successive relays of guests who come and go. There are gold and silver dishes, abundance of food and perfumes. The wise guest eats as much as is sufficient for him, smells the perfumes, thanks his host, and departs. The foolish guest, on the other hand, tries to carry off some of the gold and silver dishes, only to find them wrenched out of his hands and himself thrust forth, disappointed and disgraced.

We may close these illustrations of the deceitfulness of the world with the following short parable. Suppose a ship to arrive at a certain well-wooded island. The captain of the ship tells the passengers he will stop a few hours there, and that they can go on shore for a short time, but warns them not to delay too long. Accordingly the passengers disembark and stroll in different directions. The wisest, however, return after a short time, and, finding the ship empty, choose the most comfortable places in it. A second band of the passengers spend a somewhat longer time on the island, admiring the foliage of the trees and listening to the song of the birds. Coming on board, they find the best places in the ship already occupied, and have to content themselves with the less comfortable ones. A third party wander still farther, and, finding some brilliantly coloured stones, carry them back to the ship. Their lateness in coming on board compels them to stow themselves away in the lower parts of the ship, where they find their loads of stones, which by this time have lost all their brilliancy, very much in their way. The last group go so far in their wanderings that they get quite out of reach of the captain's voice calling them to come on board, and at last he has to sail away without them. They wander about in a hopeless condition and finally either perish of hunger or fall a prey to wild beasts.

The first group represents the faithful who keep aloof from the world altogether, and the last group the infidels who care only for this world and nothing for the next. The two intermediate classes are those who preserve their faith, but entangle themselves more or less with the vanities of things present.

Although we have said so much against the world, it must be remembered that there are some things in the world which are not *of* it, such as knowledge and good deeds. A man carries what knowledge he possesses with him into the next world, and, though his good deeds have passed, yet the effect of them remains in his character. Especially is this the case with acts of devotion, which result in the perpetual remembrance and love of God. These are among "those good things" which, as the Koran says, "pass not away."

Other good things there are in the world, such

as marriage, food, clothing, etc., which a wise man uses just in proportion as they help him to attain to the next world. Other things which engross the mind, causing it to cleave to this world and to be careless of the next, are purely evil and were alluded to by the Prophet when he said, "The world is a curse, and all which is in it is a curse, except the remembrance of God, and that which aids it."

CHAPTER IV

THE KNOWLEDGE OF THE NEXT WORLD

As regards the joys of heaven and the pains of hell which will follow this life, all believers in the Koran and the Traditions are sufficiently informed. But it often escapes them that there is also a spiritual heaven and hell, concerning the former of which God said to His Prophet, "Eye hath not seen, nor ear heard, neither hath it entered into the heart of man to conceive the things which are prepared for the righteous." In the heart of the enlightened man there is a window opening on the realities of the spiritual world, so that he knows, not by hearsay or traditional belief, but by actual experience, what produces wretchedness or happiness in the soul just as clearly and decidedly as the physician knows what produces sickness or health in the body. He recognises that knowledge of God and worship are medicinal, and that ignorance and sin are deadly poisons for the soul. Many even so-called "learned" men, from blindly following others' opinions, have no real certainty in their beliefs regarding the happiness or misery of souls in the next world, but he who will attend to the matter with a mind unbiassed by prejudice will arrive at clear convictions on this matter.

The effect of death on the composite nature of man is as follows: Man has two souls, an animal soul and a spiritual soul, which latter is of angelic nature. The seat of the animal soul is the heart, from which this soul issues like a subtle vapour and pervades all the members of the body, giving the power of sight to the eye, the power of hearing to the ear, and to every member the faculty of performing its own appropriate functions. It may be compared to a lamp carried about within a cottage, the light of which falls upon the walls wherever it goes. The heart is the wick of this lamp, and when the supply of oil is cut off for any reason, the lamp dies. Such is the death of the animal soul. With the spiritual, or human soul, the case is different. It is indivisible, and by it man knows God. It is, so to speak, the rider of the animal soul, and when that perishes it still remains, but is like a horseman who has been dismounted, or like a hunter who has lost his weapons. That steed and those weapons were granted the human soul that by means of them it might pursue and capture the Phœnix of the love and knowledge of God. If it *has* effected that capture, it is not a grief but rather a relief to be able to lay those weapons aside, and to dismount from that weary steed. Therefore the Prophet said, "Death is a welcome gift of God to the believer." But alas for that soul which loses its steed and hunting-weapons before it has captured the prize! Its misery and regret will be indescribable.

A little further consideration will show how entirely distinct the human soul is from the body and its members. Limb after limb may be paralysed and cease working, but the individuality of the soul is unimpaired. Further, the body which you have now is no longer the body which you had as a child, but entirely different, yet your Personality now is identical with your personality then. It is therefore easy to conceive of it as persisting when the body is done with altogether, along with its essential attributes which were independent of the body, such as the knowledge and love of God. This is the meaning of that saying of the Koran, "The good things abide." But if, instead of carrying away with you knowledge, you depart in ignorance of God, this ignorance also is an essential attribute, and will abide as darkness of soul and the seed of misery. Therefore the Koran says, "He who is blind in this life will be blind in the next life, and astray from the path."

The reason of the human spirit seeking to return to that upper world is that its origin was from thence, and that it is of angelic nature. It was sent down into this lower sphere against its will to acquire knowledge and experience, as God said in the Koran: "Go down from hence, all of you; there will come to you instruction from Me, and they who obey the instruction need not fear, neither shall they be grieved." The verse, "I breathed into man of My spirit," also points to the celestial origin of the human soul. Just as the health of the animal soul consists in the equilibrium of its component parts, and this equilibrium is restored, when impaired, by appropriate medicine, so the health of the human soul consists in a moral equilibrium which is maintained and repaired, when needful, by ethical instruction and moral precepts.

As regards its future existence, we have already seen that the human soul is essentially independent of the body. All objections to its existence after death based on the supposed necessity of its recovering its former body fall, therefore, to the ground. Some theologians have supposed that the human soul is annihilated after death and then restored, but this is contrary both to reason and to the Koran. The former shows us that death does not destroy the essential individuality of a man, and the Koran says, "Think not that those who are slain in the path of God are dead; nay, they are alive, rejoicing in the presence of their Lord, and in the grace bestowed on them." Not a word is said in the Law about any of the dead, good or bad, being annihilated. Nay, the Prophet is said to have questioned the spirits of slain infidels as to whether they had found the punishments, with which he had threatened them, real or not. When his followers asked him what was the good of questioning them, he replied, "They hear my words better than you do."

Some Sufis have had the unseen world of heaven and hell revealed to them when in a state of death-like trance. On their recovering consciousness their faces betray the nature of the revelations they have had by marks of joy or terror. But no visions are necessary to prove what will occur to every thinking man, that when death has stripped him of his senses and left him nothing but his bare personality, if while on earth he has too closely attached himself to objects perceived by the senses, such as wives, children, wealth, lands, slaves, male and female, etc., he must necessarily suffer when bereft of those objects. Whereas, on the contrary, if he has as far as possible turned his back on all earthly objects and fixed his supreme affection upon God, he will welcome death as a means of escape from worldly entanglements, and of union with Him whom he loves. In his case the Prophet's sayings will be verified: "Death is a bridge which unites friend to friend," and "The world is a paradise for infidels, but a prison for the faithful."

On the other hand, the pains which souls suffer after death all have their source in excessive love of the world. The Prophet said that every unbeliever, after death, will be tormented by ninety-nine snakes, each having nine heads. Some simple-minded people have examined the unbelievers' graves and wondered at failing to see these snakes. They do not understand that these snakes have their abode within the unbeliever's spirit, and that they existed in him even before he died, for they were his own evil qualities symbolised, such as jealousy, hatred, hypocrisy, pride, deceit, etc., every one of which springs, directly or remotely, from love of the world. Such is the doom of those who, in the words of the Koran, "set their hearts on this world rather than on the next." If those snakes were merely external they might hope to escape their torment, if it were but for a moment; but, being their own inherent attributes, how can they escape?

Take, for instance, the case of a man who has sold a slave-girl without knowing how much he was attached to her till she is quite out of his reach. Then the love of her, hitherto dormant, wakes up in him with such intensity as to amount to torture, stinging him like a snake, so that he would fain cast himself into fire or water to escape it. Such is the effect of love of the world, which those who have it often suspect not till the world is taken from them, and then the torment of vain longing is such that they would gladly exchange it for any number of mere external snakes and scorpions.

Every sinner thus carries with him into the world beyond death the instruments of his own punishment; and the Koran says truly, "Verily you shall see hell; you shall see it with the eye of certainty," and "hell surrounds the unbelievers." It does not say "will surround them," for it is round them even now.

Some may object, "If such is the case, then who can escape hell, for who is not more or less bound to the world by various ties of affection and interest?" To this we answer that there are some, notably the faqirs, who have entirely disengaged themselves from love of the world. But even among those who have worldly possessions such as wife, children, houses, etc., there are those who, though they have some affection for these, love God yet more. Their case is like that of a man who, though he may have a dwelling which he is fond of in one city, when he is called by the king to take up a post of authority in another city, does so gladly, as the post of authority is dearer to him than his former dwelling. Such are many of the prophets and saints.

Others there are, and a great number, who have some love to God, but the love of the world so preponderates in them that they will have to suffer a good deal of pain after death before they are thoroughly weaned from it. Many profess to love God, but a man may easily test himself by watching which way the balance of his affection inclines when the commands of God come into collision with some of his desires. The profession of love to God which is insufficient to restrain from disobedience to God is a lie.

We have seen above that one kind of spiritual hell is the forcible separation from worldly things to which the heart clave too fondly. Many carry about within them the germs of such a hell without being aware of it; hereafter they will feel like some king who, after living in luxury, has been dethroned and made a laughing-stock. The second kind of spiritual hell is that of shame, when a man wakes up to see the nature of the actions he committed in their naked reality. Thus he who slandered will see himself in the guise of a cannibal eating his dead brother's flesh, and he who envied as one who cast stones against a wall, which stones, rebounding, put out the eyes of his own children.

This species of hell, *i.e.* of shame, may be symbolised by the following short parable: Suppose a certain king has been celebrating his son's marriage. In the evening the young man goes off with some companions and presently returns to the palace (as he thinks) intoxicated. He enters a chamber where a light is burning and lies down, as he supposes, by his bride. In the morning, when soberness returns, he is aghast to find himself in a mortuary of the fire-worshippers, his couch a bier, and the form which he mistook for that of his bride the corpse of an old woman beginning to decay. On emerging from the mortuary with his garments all soiled, what is his shame to see his father, the king, approaching with a retinue of soldiers! Such is a feeble picture of the shame those will feel in the next world who in this have greedily abandoned themselves to what they thought were delights.

The third spiritual hell is that of disappointment and failure to reach the real objects of existence. Man was intended to mirror forth the light of the knowledge of God, but if he arrives in the next world with his soul thickly coated with the rust of sensual indulgence he will entirely fail of the object for which he was made. His disappointment may be figured in the following way: Suppose a man is passing with some companions through a dark wood. Here and there, glimmering on the ground, lie variously coloured stones. His companions collect and carry these and advise him to do the same. "For," say they, "we have heard that these stones will fetch a high price in the place whither we are going." He, on the other hand, laughs at them and calls them fools for loading themselves in the vain hope of gain, while he walks free and unencumbered. Presently they emerge into the full daylight and find that these coloured stones are rubies, emeralds, and other jewels of priceless value. The man's disappointment and chagrin at not having gathered some when so easily within his reach may be more easily imagined than described. Such will be the remorse of those hereafter, who, while passing through this world, have been at no pains to acquire the jewels of virtue and the treasures of religion.

This journey of man through the world may be divided into four stages—the sensuous, the experimental, the instinctive, the rational. In the first he is like a moth which, though it has sight, has no memory, and will singe itself again and again at the same candle. In the second stage he is like a dog which, having once been beaten, will run away at the sight of a stick. In the third he is like a horse or a sheep, both of which instinctively fly at the sight of a lion or a wolf, their natural enemies, while they will not fly from a camel or a buffalo, though these last are much greater in size. In the fourth stage man altogether transcends the limits of the animals and becomes capable, to some extent, of foreseeing and providing for the future. His movements at first may be compared to ordinary walking on land, then to traversing the sea in a ship, then, on the fourth plane, where he is conversant with realities, to walking on the sea, while beyond this plane there is a fifth, known to the prophets and saints, whose progress may be compared to flying through the air.

Thus man is capable of existing on several different planes, from the animal to the angelic, and precisely in this lies his danger, *i.e.* of falling to the very lowest. In the Koran it is written, "We proposed the burden (*i.e.* responsibility or free-will) to the heavens and the earth and the mountains, and they refused to undertake it. But man took it upon himself: Verily he is ignorant." Neither animals nor angels can change their appointed rank and place. But man may sink to the animal or soar to the angel, and this is the meaning of his undertaking that "burden" of which the Koran speaks. The majority of men choose to remain in the two lower stages mentioned above, and the stationary are always hostile to the travellers or pilgrims, whom they far outnumber.

Many of the former class, having no fixed convictions about the future world, when mastered by their sensual appetites, deny it altogether. They say that hell is merely an invention of theologians to frighten people, and they regard theologians themselves with thinly veiled contempt. To argue with fools of this kind is of very little use. This much, however, may be said to such a man, with the possible result of making him pause and reflect: "Do you really think that the hundred and twenty-four thousand[1] prophets and saints who believed in the future life were all wrong, and you are right in denying it?" If he replies, "Yes! I am as sure as I am that two are more than one, that there is no soul and no future life of joy and penalty," then the case of such a man is hopeless; all one can do is to leave him alone, remembering the words of the Koran, "Though thou call them to instruction, they will not be instructed."

But, should he say that a future life is possible but that the doctrine is so involved in doubt and mystery that it is impossible to decide whether it be true or not, then one may say to him: "Then you had better give it the benefit of the doubt! Suppose you are about to eat food and some one tells you a serpent has spat venom on it, you would probably refrain and rather endure the pangs of hunger than eat it, though your informant may be in jest or lying. Or suppose you are ill and a charm-writer says, 'Give me a rupee and I will write a charm which you can tie round your neck and which will cure you,' you would probably give the rupee on the chance of deriving benefit from the charm. Or if an astrologer say, 'When the moon has entered a certain constellation, drink such and such a medicine, and you will recover,' though you

[1] The number of prophets according to Muhammadan tradition.

may have very little faith in astrology, you very likely would try the experiment on the chance that he might be right. And do you not think that reliance is as well placed on the words of all the prophets, saints, and holy men, convinced as they were of a future life, as on the promise of a charm-writer or an astrologer? People take perilous voyages in ships for the sake of merely probable profit, and will you not suffer a little pain of abstinence now for the sake of eternal joy hereafter?"

The Lord Ali once, in arguing with an unbeliever, said, "If you are right, then neither of us will be any the worse in the future; but if we are right, then we shall escape, and you will suffer." This he said not because he himself was in any doubt, but merely to make an impression on the unbeliever. From all that we have said it follows that man's chief business in this world is to prepare for the next. Even if he is doubtful about a future existence, reason suggests that he should act as if there were one, considering the tremendous issues at stake. Peace be on those who follow the instruction!

CHAPTER V

CONCERNING MUSIC AND DANCING AS AIDS TO THE RELIGIOUS LIFE

THE heart of man has been so constituted by the Almighty that, like a flint, it contains a hidden fire which is evoked by music and harmony, and renders man beside himself with ecstasy. These harmonies are echoes of that higher world of beauty which we call the world of spirits; they remind man of his relationship to that world, and produce in him an emotion so deep and strange that he himself is powerless to explain it. The effect of music and dancing is deeper in proportion as the natures on which they act are simple and prone to emotion; they fan into a flame whatever love is already dormant in the heart, whether it be earthly and sensual, or divine and spiritual.

Accordingly there has been much dispute among theologians as to the lawfulness of music and dancing regarded as religious exercises. One sect, the Zahirites,[1] holding that God is altogether

[1] Literally, "Outsiders."

incommensurable with man, deny the possibility of man's really feeling love to God, and say that he can only love those of his own species. If he *does* feel what he thinks is love to his Creator they say it is a mere projection, or shadow cast by his own fantasy, or a reflection of love to the creature; music and dancing, according to them, have only to do with creature love, and are therefore unlawful as religious exercises. If we ask them what is the meaning of that "love to God" which is enjoined by the religious law, they reply that it means obedience and worship. This is an error which we hope to confute in a later chapter dealing with the love of God. At present we content ourselves with saying that music and dancing do not put into the heart what is not there already, but only fan into a flame dormant emotions. Therefore if a man has in his heart that love to God which the Law enjoins it is perfectly lawful, nay, laudable in him to take part in exercises which promote it. On the other hand, if his heart is full of sensual desires, music and dancing will only increase them, and are therefore unlawful for him. While, if he listens to them merely as a matter of amusement, they are neither lawful nor unlawful, but indifferent. For the mere fact that they are pleasant does not make them unlawful, any more than the pleasure of listening to the singing of birds or looking at green grass and running water is unlawful. The innocent character of music and dancing, regarded merely as a pastime, is also corroborated by an authentic tradition which we have from the Lady Ayesha,[1] who narrates: "One festival-day some negroes were performing in a mosque. The Prophet said to me, 'Do you wish to see them?' I replied, 'Yes.' Accordingly he lifted me up with his own blessed hand, and I looked on so long that he said more than once, 'Haven't you had enough?'" Another tradition from the Lady Ayesha is as follows: "One festival-day two girls came to my house and began to play and sing. The Prophet came in and lay down on the couch, turning his face away. Presently Abu Bakr[2] entered, and, seeing the girls playing, exclaimed, 'What! the pipe of Satan in the Prophet's house!' Whereupon the Prophet turned and said, 'Let them alone, Abu Bakr, for this is a festival-day.'"

Passing over the cases where music and dancing rouse into a flame evil desires already dormant in the heart, we come to those cases where they are quite lawful. Such are those of the pilgrims who celebrate the glories of the House of God at Mecca in song, and thus incite others to go on pilgrimage, and of minstrels whose music and songs stir up martial ardour in the breasts of their auditors and incite them to fight against

[1] Muhammad's favourite wife.
[2] Subsequently the first caliph.

the infidels. Similarly, mournful music which excites sorrow for sin and failure in the religious life is lawful; of this nature was the music of David. But dirges which increase sorrow for the dead are not lawful, for it is written in the Koran, "Despair not over what you have lost." On the other hand, joyful music at weddings and feasts and on such occasions as a circumcision or the return from a journey is lawful.

We come now to the purely religious use of music and dancing: such is that of the Sufis, who by this means stir up in themselves greater love towards God, and, by means of music, often obtain spiritual visions and ecstasies, their heart becoming in this condition as clean as silver in the flame of a furnace, and attaining a degree of purity which could never be attained by any amount of mere outward austerities. The Sufi then becomes so keenly aware of his relationship to the spiritual world that he loses all consciousness of this world, and often falls down senseless.

It is not, however, lawful for the aspirant to Sufiism to take part in this mystical dancing without the permission of his "Pir," or spiritual director. It is related of the Sheikh Abu'l Qasim Girgani that, when one of his disciples requested leave to take part in such a dance, he said, "Keep a strict fast for three days; then let them cook for you tempting dishes; if, then, you still prefer the 'dance,' you may take part in it." The disciple, however, whose heart is not thoroughly purged from earthly desires, though he may have obtained some glimpse of the mystics' path, should be forbidden by his director to take part in such dances, as they will do him more harm than good.

Those who deny the reality of the ecstasies and other spiritual experiences of the Sufis merely betray their own narrow-mindedness and shallow insight. Some allowance, however, must be made for them, for it is as difficult to believe in the reality of states of which one has no personal experience as it is for a blind man to understand the pleasure of looking at green grass and running water, or for a child to comprehend the pleasure of exercising sovereignty. A wise man, though he himself may have no experience of those states, will not therefore deny their reality, for what folly can be greater than his who denies the reality of a thing merely because he himself has not experienced it! Of such people it is written in the Koran, "Those who have not the guidance will say, 'This is a manifest imposture.'"

As regards the erotic poetry which is recited in Sufi gatherings, and to which people sometimes make objection, we must remember that, when in such poetry mention is made of separation from or union with the beloved, the Sufi, who is an adept in the love of God, applies such expressions to separation from or union with Him.

Similarly, "dark locks" are taken to signify the darkness of unbelief; "the brightness of the face" the light of faith, and drunkenness the Sufi's ecstasy. Take, for instance, the verse:

Thou may'st measure out thousands of measures of wine,
But, till thou *drink* it, no joy is thine.

By this the writer means that the true delights of religion cannot be reached by way of formal instruction, but by felt attraction and desire. A man may converse much and write volumes concerning love, faith, piety, and so forth, and blacken paper to any extent, but till he himself possesses these attributes all this will do him no good. Thus, those who find fault with the Sufis for being powerfully affected, even to ecstasy, by these and similar verses, are merely shallow and uncharitable. Even camels are sometimes so powerfully affected by the Arab-songs of their drivers that they will run rapidly, bearing heavy burdens, till they fall down in a state of exhaustion.

The Sufi hearer, however, is in danger of blasphemy if he applies some of the verses which he hears to God. For instance, if he hears such a verse as "Thou art changed from thy former inclination," he must not apply it to God, who cannot change, but to himself and his own variations of mood. God is like the sun, which is always shining, but sometimes for us His light is eclipsed by some object which intervenes between us and Him.

Regarding some adepts it is related that they attain to such a degree of ecstasy that they lose themselves in God. Such was the case with Sheikh Abu'l Hassan Nuri, who, on hearing a certain verse, fell into an ecstatic condition, and, coming into a field full of stalks of newly cut sugar-canes, ran about till his feet were wounded and bleeding, and, not long afterwards, expired. In such cases some have supposed that there occurs an actual descent of Deity into humanity, but this would be as great a mistake as that of one who, having for the first time seen his reflection in a mirror, should suppose that, somehow or other, he had become incorporated with the mirror, or that the red-and-white hues which the mirror reflects were qualities inherent in it.

The states of ecstasy into which the Sufis fall vary according to the emotions which predominate in them—love, fear, desire, repentance, etc. These states, as we have mentioned above, are often the result not only of hearing verses of the Koran, but erotic poetry. Some have objected to the reciting of poetry, as well as of the Koran, on these occasions; but it should be remembered that all the verses of the Koran are not adapted to stir the emotions—such, for instance, as that which commands that a man should leave his mother the sixth part of his property and his sister the half, or that which orders that a widow must wait four months after the death of her husband before becoming espoused to another man. The natures which can be thrown into religious ecstasy by the recital of such verses are peculiarly sensitive and very rare.

Another reason for the use of poetry as well as of the Koran on these occasions is that people are so familiar with the Koran, many even knowing it by heart, that the effect of it has been dulled by constant repetition. One cannot be always quoting new verses of the Koran as one can of poetry. Once, when some wild Arabs were hearing the Koran for the first time and were strongly moved by it, Abu-Bakr said to them, "We were once like you, but our hearts have grown hard," meaning that the Koran loses some of its effect on those familiar with it. For the same reason the Caliph Omar used to command the pilgrims to Mecca to leave it quickly, "For," he said, "I fear if you grow too familiar with the Holy City the awe of it will depart from your hearts."

There is, moreover, something pertaining to the light and frivolous, at least in the eyes of the common people, in the use of singing and musical instruments, such as the pipe and drum, and it is not befitting that the majesty of the Koran should be, even temporarily, associated with these things. It is related of the Prophet that once, when he entered the house of Rabia, the daughter of Mauz, some singing-girls who were there began extemporising in his honour. He abruptly bade them cease, as the praise of the Prophet was too sacred a theme to be treated in that way. There is also some danger, if verses of the Koran are exclusively used, that the hearers should attach to them some private interpretation of their own, and this is unlawful. On the other hand, no harm attaches to interpreting lines of poetry in various ways, as it is not necessary to apply to a poem the same meaning which the author had.

Other features of these mystic dances are the bodily contortions and tearing of clothes with which they are sometimes accompanied. If these are the result of genuine ecstatic conditions there is nothing to be said against them, but if they are self-conscious and deliberate on the part of those who wish to appear "adepts," then they are merely acts of hypocrisy. In any case the more perfect adept is he who controls himself till he is absolutely obliged to give vent to his feelings. It is related of a certain youth who was a disciple of the Sheikh Junaid that, on hearing singing commence in an assembly of the Sufis, he could not restrain himself, but began to shriek in ecstasy. Junaid said to him, "If you do that again, don't remain in my company."

After this the youth used to restrain himself on such occasions, but at last one day his emotions were so powerfully stirred that, after long and forcible repression of them, he uttered a shriek and died.

To conclude: in holding these assemblies, regard must be had to time and place, and that no spectators come from unworthy motives. Those who participate in them should sit in silence, not looking at one another, but keeping their heads bent, as at prayer, and concentrating their minds on God. Each should watch for whatever may be revealed to his own heart, and not make any movements from mere self-conscious impulse. But if any one of them stands up in a state of genuine ecstasy all the rest should stand up with him, and if any one's turban fall off the others should also lay their turbans down.

Although these matters are comparative novelties in Islam and have not been received from the first followers of the Prophet, we must remember that all novelties are not forbidden, but only those which directly contravene the Law. For instance, the "Tarawih," or night-prayer, was first instituted by the Caliph Omar. The Prophet said, "Live with each man according to his habits and disposition," therefore it is right to fall in with usages that please people, when non-conformity would vex them. It is true that the Companions were not in the habit of rising on the entrance of the Prophet, as they disliked this practice; but where it has become established, and abstaining from it would cause annoyance, it is better to conform to it. The Arabs have their own customs, and the Persians have theirs, and God knoweth which is best.

CHAPTER VI

CONCERNING SELF-EXAMINATION AND THE RECOLLECTION OF GOD

KNOW, O brother, that in the Koran God hath said, "We will set up a just balance on the day of resurrection, and no soul shall be wronged in anything." Whosoever has wrought a grain of good or ill shall then behold it. In the Koran it is also written, "Let every soul see what it sends on before it for the day of account." It was a saying of the Caliph Omar's, "Call yourselves to account before ye be called to account"; and God says, "O ye believers, be patient and strive against your natural desires, and maintain the strife manfully." The saints have always understood that they have come into this world to carry on a spiritual traffic, the resulting gain or loss of which is heaven or hell. They have, therefore, always kept a jealous eye upon the flesh, which, like a treacherous partner in business, may cause them great loss. He, therefore, is a wise man who, after his morning prayer, spends a whole hour in making a spiritual reckoning, and says to his soul, "O my soul, thou hast only one life; no single moment that has passed can be recovered, for in the counsel of God the number of breaths allotted thee is fixed, and cannot be increased. When life is over no further spiritual traffic is possible for thee; therefore what thou doest, do now; treat this day as if thy life had been already spent, and this were an extra day granted thee by the special favour of the Almighty. What can be greater folly than to lose it?"

At the resurrection a man will find all the hours of his life arranged like a long series of treasure-chests. The door of one will be opened, and it will be seen to be full of light: it represents an hour which he spent in doing good. His heart will be filled with such joy that even a fraction of it would make the inhabitants of hell forget the fire. The door of a second will be opened; it is pitch-dark within, and from it issues such an evil odour as will cause every one to hold his nose: it represents an hour which he spent in ill-doing, and he will suffer such terror that a fraction of it would embitter Paradise for the blessed. The door of a third treasure-chest will be opened; it will be seen to be empty and neither light nor dark within: this represents the hour in which he did neither good nor evil. Then he will feel remorse and confusion like that of a man who has been the possessor of a great treasure and wasted it or let it slip from his grasp. Thus the whole series of the hours of his life will be displayed, one by one, to his gaze. Therefore a man should say to his soul every morning, "God has given thee twenty-four treasures; take heed lest thou lose any one of them, for thou wilt not be able to endure the regret that will follow such loss."

The saints have said, "Even suppose God should forgive thee, after a wasted life, thou wilt not attain to the ranks of the righteous and must deplore thy loss; therefore keep a strict watch over thy tongue, thine eye, and each of thy seven members, for each of these is, as it were, a possible gate to hell. Say to thy flesh, 'If thou art rebellious, verily I will punish thee'; for, though the flesh is headstrong, it is capable of receiving instruction, and can be tamed by austerity." Such, then, is the aim of self-examination, and the Prophet has said, "Happy is he who does now that which will benefit him after death."

We come now to the recollection of God. This consists in a man's remembering that God observes all his acts and thoughts. People only see the outward, while God sees both the outer and the inner man. He who really believes this will have both his outer and inner being well disciplined. If he disbelieve it, he is an infidel, and if, while believing it, he acts contrary to that belief, he is guilty of the grossest presumption. One day a negro came to the Prophet and said, "O Prophet of God! I have committed much sin. Will my repentance be accepted, or not?" The Prophet said "Yes." Then the negro said, "O Prophet of God, all the time I was committing sin, did God really behold it?" "Yes," was the answer. The negro uttered a cry and fell lifeless. Till a man is thoroughly convinced of the fact that he is always under God's observation it is impossible for him to act rightly.

A certain sheikh once had a disciple whom he favoured above his other disciples, thus exciting their envy. One day the sheikh gave each of them a fowl and told each to go and kill it in a place where no one could see him. Accordingly each killed his fowl in some retired spot and brought it back, with the exception of the sheikh's favourite disciple, who brought his back alive, saying, "I have found no such place, for God sees everywhere." The sheikh said to the others, "You see now this youth's real rank; he has attained to the constant remembrance of God."

When Zuleikha tempted Joseph she cast a cloth over the face of the idol she used to worship. Joseph said to her, "O Zuleikha, thou art ashamed before a block of stone, and should I not be ashamed before Him who created the seven heavens and the earth?" A man once came to the saint Junaid and said, "I cannot keep my eyes from casting lascivious looks. How shall I do so?" "By remembering," Junaid answered, "that God sees you much more clearly than you see any one else." In the traditions it is written that God has said, "Paradise is for those who intend to commit some sin and then remember that My eye is upon them and forbear." Abdullah Ibn Dinar relates, "Once I was walking with the Caliph Omar near Mecca when we met a shepherd's slave-boy driving his flock. Omar said to him, "Sell me a sheep." The boy answered, "They are not mine, but my master's." Then, to try him, Omar said, "Well, you can tell him that a wolf carried one off, and he will know nothing about it." "No, he won't," said the boy, "but God will." Omar then wept, and, sending for the boy's master, purchased him and set him free, exclaiming, "For this saying thou art free in this world and shalt be free in the next."

There are two degrees of this recollection of God. The first degree is that of those saints whose thoughts are altogether absorbed in the contemplation of the majesty of God, and have no room in their hearts for anything else at all. This is the lower degree of recollection, for when a man's heart is fixed, and his limbs are so controlled by his heart that they abstain from even lawful actions, he has no need of any device or safeguard against sins. It was to this kind of recollection that the Prophet referred when he said, "He who rises in the morning with only God in his mind, God shall look after him, both in this world and the next."

Some of these recollectors of God are so absorbed in the thought of Him that, if people speak to them they do not hear, or walk in front of them they do not see, but stumble as if they collided with a wall. A certain saint relates as follows: "One day I passed by a place where archers were having a shooting-match. Some way off a man was sitting alone. I approached him and attempted to engage him in talk, but he replied, "The remembrance of God is better than talk." I said, "Are you not lonely?" "No," he answered, "God and two angels are with me." Pointing to the archers, I asked, "Which of these has carried off the prize?" "That one,' was his reply, "to whom God has allotted it." Then I inquired, "Where does this road come from?" Upon which, lifting up his eyes to heaven, he rose and departed, saying, "O Lord! many of Thy creatures hold one back from the remembrance of Thee!"

The saint Shibli one day went to see the Sufi Thaury; he found him sitting so still in contemplation that not a hair of his body moved. He asked him, "From whom didst thou learn to practise such fixity of contemplation?" Thaury answered, "From a cat which I saw waiting at a mouse-hole in an attitude of even greater fixity than this." Ibn Hanif relates: "I was informed that in the city of Sur a sheikh and his disciple were always sitting lost in the recollection of God. I went there and found them both sitting with their faces turned in the direction of Mecca. I saluted them thrice, but they gave no answer. I said, 'I adjure you, by God, to return my salutation.'[1] The youth raised his head and replied, 'O Ibn Hanif! The world lasts but for a little time, and of this little time only a little is remaining. Thou art hindering us by requiring us to return thy salutation.' He then bent his head again and was silent. I was hungry and thirsty at the time, but the sight of those two quite carried me out of myself. I remained standing and prayed with them the afternoon and evening prayer. I then asked them for some spiritual advice. The younger replied, 'O Ibn Hanif, we are afflicted; we do not possess that tongue which gives advice.' I remained standing there three days and nights; no word passed between us and none of us slept. Then I said within myself, 'I will adjure them by God to give me some counsel.' The younger, divining my thoughts, again raised his head: 'Go and seek such a man, the visitation of whom will bring God to thy remembrance and infix His

[1] A Moslem is bound by the Koran to return the salutation of a Moslem.

fear in thy heart, and he will give thee that counsel which is conveyed by silence and not by speech.' "

Such is the "recollection" of the saints which consists in being entirely absorbed in the contemplation of God. The second degree of the recollection of God is that of "the companions of the right hand."[1] These are aware that God knows all about them, and feel abashed in His presence, yet they are not carried out of themselves by the thought of His majesty, but remain clearly conscious of themselves and of the world. Their condition is like that of a man who should be suddenly surprised in a state of nakedness and should hastily cover himself, while the other class resemble one who suddenly finds himself in the presence of the King and is confused and awestruck. The former subject every project which enters their minds to a thorough scrutiny, for at the Last Day three questions will be asked respecting every action: the first, "Why did you do this?" the second, "In what way did you do this?" the third, "For what purpose did you do this?" The first will be asked because a man should act from divine and not merely Satanic or fleshly impulse. If this question is satisfactorily answered, the second will test in what way the action was done, wisely, or carelessly and negligently, and the third, whether

[1] Koranic phrase for the righteous.

it was done simply to please God, or to gain the approval of men. If a man understands the meaning of these questions he will be very watchful over the state of his heart, and how he entertains thoughts which are likely to end in action. Rightly to discriminate among such thoughts is a very difficult and delicate matter, and he who is not capable of it should attach himself to some spiritual director, intercourse with whom may illuminate his heart. He should avoid with the utmost care the merely worldly learned man who is an agent of Satan. God said to David, "O David! ask no questions of the learned man who is intoxicated with love of the world, for he will rob thee of My love," and the Prophet said: "God loves that man who is keen to discern in doubtful things, and who suffers not his reason to be swayed by the assaults of passion." Reason and discrimination are closely connected, and he in whom reason does not rule passion will not be keen to discriminate.

Besides such cautious discrimination before acting a man should call himself strictly to account for his past actions. Every evening he should examine his heart as to what he has done to see whether he has gained or lost in his spiritual capital. This is the more necessary as the heart is like a treacherous business-partner, always ready to cajole and deceive; sometimes it presents its own selfishness under the guise of obedience to God, so that a man supposes he has gained, whereas he has really lost.

A certain saint named Amiya, sixty years of age, counted up the days of his life. He found they amounted to twenty-one thousand six hundred days. He said to himself, "Alas! if I have committed one sin every day, how can I escape from the load of twenty-one thousand six hundred sins?" He uttered a cry and fell to the ground; when they came to raise him they found him dead. But most people are heedless, and never think of calling themselves to account. If for every sin a man committed he placed a stone in an empty house, he would soon find that house full of stones; if his recording angels[1] demanded wages of him for writing down his sins, all his money would soon be gone. People count on their rosaries[2] with self-satisfaction the numbers of times they have recited the name of God, but they keep no rosary for reckoning the numberless idle words they speak. Therefore the Caliph Omar said, "Weigh well your words and deeds before they be weighed at the Judgment." He himself, before retiring for the night, used to strike his feet with a scourge and exclaim, "What hast thou done to-day?" Abu Talha was once praying in a palm-grove, when the sight of a

[1] Two of these are attached to every man.

[2] The Muhammadan rosary consists of ninety-nine beads; each representing a name of God.

beautiful bird which flew out of it caused him to make a mistake in counting the number of prostrations he had made. To punish himself for his inattention, he gave the palm-grove away. Such saints knew that their sensual nature was prone to go astray, therefore they kept a strict watch over it, and punished it for each transgression.

If a man finds himself sluggish and averse from austerity and self-discipline he should consort with one who is a proficient in such practices so as to catch the contagion of his enthusiasm. One saint used to say, "When I grow lukewarm in self-discipline, I look at Muhammad Ibn Wasi, and the sight of him rekindles my fervour for at least a week." If one cannot find such a pattern of austerity close at hand, then it is a good thing to study the lives of the saints; he should also exhort his soul somewhat in the following way: "O my soul! thou thinkest thyself intelligent and art angry at being called a fool, and yet what else art thou, after all? Thou preparest clothing to shield thee from the cold of winter, yet makest no preparation for the after-life. Thy state is like that of a man who in mid-winter should say, 'I will wear no warm clothing, but trust to God's mercy to shield me from the cold. He forgets that God, at the same time that He created cold, showed man the way to make clothing to protect himself from it, and provided the material for that clothing. Remember this also, O soul, that thy punishment hereafter will not be because God is angry with thy disobedience; and say not, 'How can my sin hurt God?' It is thy lusts themselves which will have kindled the flames of hell within thee; just as, from eating unwholesome food, disease is caused in a man's body, and not because his doctor is vexed with him for disobeying his orders.

"Shame upon thee, O soul, for thy overweening love of the world! If thou dost not believe in heaven or hell, at any rate thou believest in death, which will snatch from thee all worldly delights and cause thee to feel the pangs of separation from them, which will be intenser just in proportion as thou hast attached thyself to them. Why art thou mad after the world? If the whole of it, from East to West, were thine and worshipped thee, yet it would all, in a brief space, turn to dust along with thyself, and oblivion would blot out thy name, as those of ancient kings before thee. But now, seeing thou hast only a very small fragment of the world, and that a defiled one, wilt thou be so mad as to barter eternal joy for it, a precious jewel for a broken cup of earthenware, and make thyself the laughing-stock of all around thee?"

CHAPTER VII

MARRIAGE AS A HELP OR HINDRANCE TO THE RELIGIOUS LIFE

MARRIAGE plays such a large part in human affairs that it must necessarily be taken into account in treating of the religious life and be regarded in both its aspects of advantage and disadvantage.

Seeing that God, as the Koran says, "only created men and genii for the purpose of worshipping," the first and obvious advantage of marriage is, that the worshippers of God may increase in number. Theologians have therefore laid it down as a maxim that it is better to be engaged in matrimonial duties than in supererogatory devotions.

Another advantage of marriage is that, as the Prophet said, the prayers of children profit their parents when the latter are dead, and children who die before their parents intercede for them on the Day of Judgment. "When a child," said the Prophet, "is told to enter heaven, it weeps and says, 'I will not enter in without my father and mother.'" Again, one day the Prophet seized hold of a man's sleeves and drew him violently towards himself, saying, "Even thus shall children draw their parents into heaven." He added, "Children crowd together at the gate of heaven and cry out for their fathers and mothers, till those of the latter who are outside are told to enter in and join their children."

It is related of a certain celibate saint that he once dreamt that the Judgment Day had come. The sun had approached close to the earth and people were perishing of thirst; a crowd of boys were moving about giving them water out of gold and silver vessels. But when the saint asked for water he was repulsed, and one of the boys said to him, "Not one of us here is your son." As soon as the saint awoke he made preparations to marry.

Another advantage of marriage is that to sit with and be friendly to one's wife is a relaxation for the mind after being occupied in religious duties, and after such relaxation one may return to one's devotions with renewed zest. Thus the Prophet himself, when he found the weight of his revelations press too heavily upon him touched his wife Ayesha and said, "Speak to me, O Ayesha, speak to me!" This he did that, from that familiar human touch, he might receive strength to support fresh revelations. For a similar reason he used to bid the Muezzin Bilal give the call to prayer, and sometimes he used to smell sweet perfumes. It is a well-known saying of his, "I have loved three things in the world: perfumes, and women, and refreshment in prayer." On one occasion Omar asked the prophet what were the things specially to be sought in the world. He answered, "A tongue occupied in the remembrance of God, a grateful heart, and a believing wife."

A further advantage of marriage is that there should be some one to take care of the house, cook the food, wash the dishes, and sweep the floor, etc. If a man is busy in such work he cannot acquire learning, or carry on his business, or engage in his devotions properly. For this reason Abu Suleiman has said, "A good wife is not a blessing of this world merely, but of the next, because she provides a man leisure in which to think of the next world"; and one of the Caliph Omar's sayings is, "After faith, no blessing is equal to a good wife."

Marriage has, moreover, this good in it, that to be patient with feminine peculiarities, to provide the necessaries which wives require, and to keep them in the path of the law, is a very important part of religion. The Prophet said, "To give one's wife the money she requires is more important than to give alms." Once, when Ibn

Mubarak was engaged in a campaign against the infidels, one of his companions asked him, "Is any work more meritorious than religious war?" "Yes," he replied: "to feed and clothe one's wife and children properly." The celebrated saint Bishr Hafi said, "It is better that a man should work for wife and children than merely for himself." In the Traditions it has been recorded that some sins can only be atoned for by enduring trouble for the sake of one's family.

Concerning a certain saint it is related that his wife died and he would not marry again, though people urged him, saying it was easier to concentrate his thoughts in solitude. One night he saw in a dream the door of heaven opened and numbers of angels descending. They came near and looked upon him, and one said, "Is this that selfish wretch?" and his fellow answered, "Yes, this is he." The saint was too alarmed to ask whom they meant, but presently a boy passed and he asked him. "It is you they are speaking about," replied the boy; "only up to a week ago your good works were being recorded in heaven along with those of other saints, but now they have erased your name from the roll." Greatly disturbed in mind as soon as he awoke, he hastened to be married. From all the above considerations it will be seen that marriage is desirable.

We come now to treat of the drawbacks to marriage. One of these is that there is a danger, especially in the present time, that a man should gain a livelihood by unlawful means in order to support his family, and no amount of good works can compensate for this. The Prophet said that at the resurrection a certain man with a whole mountain-load of good works will be brought forward and stationed near the Balance.[1] He will then be asked, "'By what means did you support your family?' He will not be able to give a satisfactory answer, and all his good works will be cancelled, and proclamation will be made concerning him, 'This is the man whose family have devoured all his good deeds!'"

Another drawback to marriage is this, that to treat one's family kindly and patiently and to bring their affairs to a satisfactory issue can only be done by those who have a good disposition. There is great danger lest a man should treat his family harshly, or neglect them, and so bring sin upon himself. The Prophet said: "He who deserts his wife and children is like a runaway slave; till he returns to them none of his fasts or prayers will be accepted by God." In brief, man has a lower nature, and, till he can control his own lower nature, he had better not assume the responsibility of controlling another's. Some

[1] The Mizan, or Balance for weighing good and evil deeds, which will be erected on the Judgment Day.

one asked the saint Bishr Hafi why he did not marry. "I am afraid," he replied, "of that verse in the Koran, 'The rights of women over men are precisely the same as the rights of men over women.'"

A third disadvantage of marriage is that the cares of a family often prevent a man from concentrating his thoughts on God and on a future life, and may, unless he is careful, lead to his destruction, for God has said, "Let not your wives and children turn you away from remembering God." He who thinks he can concentrate himself better on his religious duties by not marrying had better remain single, and he who fears falling into sin if he does not marry, had better do so.

We now come to the qualities which should be sought in a wife. The most important of all is chastity. If a wife is unchaste, and her husband keeps silent, he gets a bad name and is hindered in his religious life; if he speaks, his life becomes embittered; and if he divorces her, he may feel the pang of separation. A wife who is beautiful but of evil character is a great calamity; such a one had better be divorced. The Prophet said, "He who seeks a wife for the sake of her beauty or wealth will lose both."

The second desirable quality in a wife is a good disposition. An ill-tempered or ungrateful or loquacious or imperious wife makes existence unbearable, and is a great hindrance to leading a devout life.

The third quality to be sought is beauty, as this calls forth love and affection. Therefore one should see a woman before marrying her. The Prophet said, "The women of such a tribe have all a defect in their eyes; he who wishes to marry one should see her first." The wise have said that he who marries a wife without seeing her is sure to repent it afterwards. It is true that one should not marry solely for the sake of beauty, but this does not mean that beauty should be reckoned of no account at all.

The fourth desirable point is that the sum paid by the husband as the wife's marriage-portion should be moderate. The Prophet said, "She is the best kind of wife whose marriage-portion is small, and whose beauty is great." He himself settled the marriage-portion of some women at ten dirhems,[1] and his own daughters' marriage-portions were not more than four hundred dirhems.

Fifthly, she should not be barren. "A piece of old matting lying in the corner of the house is better than a barren wife."[2]

Other qualities in a desirable wife are these: she should be of a good stock, not married previously, and not too nearly related to her husband.

[1] The dirhem = about sixpence.
[2] Saying of Muhammad.

Regarding the Observances of Marriage

Marriage is a religious institution, and should be treated in a religious way, otherwise the mating of men and women is no better than the mating of animals. The Law enjoins that there should be a feast on the occasion of every marriage. When Abdurrahman Ibn Auf married, the Prophet said to him, "Make a marriage-feast, even if you have only a goat to make it with." When the Prophet himself celebrated his marriage with Safia he made a marriage-feast of dates and barley. It is also right that marriage should be accompanied with the beating of drums and of music, for man is the crown of creation.

Secondly, a man should remain on good terms with his wife. This does not mean that he should never cause her pain, but that he should bear any annoyance she causes him, whether by her unreasonableness or ingratitude, patiently. Woman is created weak, and requiring concealment; she should therefore be borne with patiently, and kept secluded. The Prophet said, "He who bears the ill-humour of his wife patiently will earn as much merit as Job did by the patient endurance of his trials." On his death-bed also he was heard to say, "Continue in prayer and treat your wives well, for they are your prisoners." He himself used to bear patiently the tempers of his wives. One day Omar's wife was angry and scolded him. He said to her, "Thou evil-tongued one, dost thou answer me back?" She replied, "Yes! the Lord of the prophets is better than thou, and his wives answer him back." He replied, "Alas for Hafsa [Omar's daughter and Muhammad's wife] if she does not humble herself"; and when he met her he said, "Take care not to answer the Prophet back." The Prophet also said, "The best of you is he who is best to his own family, as I am the best to mine."

Thirdly, a man should condescend to his wife's recreations and amusements, and not attempt to check them. The Prophet himself actually on one occasion ran races with his young wife Ayesha. The first time he beat her, and the second time she beat him. Another time he held her up in his arms that she might look at some performing negroes. In fact, it would be difficult to find any one who was so kind to his wives as the Prophet was to his. Wise men have said, "A man should come home smiling and eat what he finds and not ask for anything he does not find." However, he should not be over-indulgent, lest his wife lose her respect for him. If he sees anything plainly wrong on her part, he should not ignore but rebuke it, or he will become a laughing-stock. In the Koran it is written, "Men should have the upper hand over women," and the Prophet said, "Woe to the man who is the servant of his wife," for she should be his servant. Wise men have said, "Consult women, and act the contrary to what they advise." In truth there is something perverse in women, and if they are allowed even a little licence, they get out of control altogether, and it is difficult to reduce them to order again. In dealing with them one should endeavour to use a mixture of severity and tenderness, with a greater proportion of the latter. The Prophet said, "Woman was formed of a crooked rib; if you try to bend her, you will break her; if you leave her alone, she will grow more and more crooked; therefore treat her tenderly."

As regards propriety, one cannot be too careful not to let one's wife look at or be looked at by a stranger, for the beginning of all mischief is in the eye. As far as possible, she should not be allowed out of the house, nor to go on the roof, nor to stand at the door. Care should be taken, however, not to be unreasonably jealous and strict. The Prophet one day asked his daughter Fatima, "What is the best thing for women?" She answered, "They should not look on strangers, nor strangers on them." The Prophet was pleased at this remark, and embraced her, saying, "Verily, thou art a piece of my liver!" The Commander of the Faithful, Omar, said, "Don't give women fine clothes, for as soon as they have them they will want to go out of the house." In the time of the Prophet women had permission to go to the mosques and stand in the last row of the worshippers; but this was subsequently forbidden.

A man should keep his wife properly supplied with money, and not stint her. To give a wife her proper maintenance is more meritorious than to give alms. The Prophet said, "Suppose a man spends one dinar[1] in religious war, another in ransoming a slave, a third in charity, and gives the fourth to his wife, the giving of this last surpasses in merit all the others put together."

A man should not eat anything especially good by himself, or, if he has eaten it, he should keep silent about it and not praise it before his wife. It is better for husband and wife to eat together, if a guest be not present, for the Prophet said, "When they do so, God sends His blessing upon them, and the angels pray for them." The most important point to see to is that the supplies given to one's wife are acquired by lawful means.

If a man's wife be rebellious and disobedient, he should at first admonish her gently; if this is not sufficient he should sleep in a separate chamber for three nights. Should this also fail he may strike her, but not on the mouth, nor with such force as to wound her. Should she be remiss in her religious duties, he should manifest

[1] About ten shillings.

his displeasure to her for an entire month, as the Prophet did on one occasion to all his wives.

The greatest care should be taken to avoid divorce, for, though divorce is permitted, yet God disapproves of it, because the very utterance of the word "divorce" causes a woman pain, and how can it be right to pain any one? When divorce is absolutely necessary, the formula for it should not be repeated thrice all at once, but on three different occasions.[1] A woman should be divorced kindly, not through anger and contempt, and not without a reason. After divorce a man should give his former wife a present, and not tell others that she has been divorced for such and such a fault. Of a certain man who was instituting divorce-proceedings against his wife it is related that people asked him, "Why are you divorcing her?" He answered, "I do not reveal my wife's secrets." When he had actually divorced her, he was asked again, and said, "She is a stranger to me now; I have nothing to do with her private affairs."

Hitherto we have treated of the rights of the wife over her husband, but the rights of the husband over the wife are even more binding. The Prophet said, "If it were right to worship any one except God, it would be right for wives to worship their husbands." A wife should not

[1] The formula for divorce has to be repeated thrice to make it complete.

boast of her beauty before her husband, she should not requite his kindness with ingratitude, she should not say to him, "Why have you treated me thus and thus?" The Prophet said, "I looked into hell and saw many women there; I asked the reason, and received this reply, 'Because they abused their husbands and were ungrateful to them.'"

CHAPTER VIII

THE LOVE OF GOD

THE love of God is the highest of all topics, and is the final aim to which we have been tending hitherto. We have spoken of spiritual dangers as they hinder the love of God in a man's heart, and we have spoken of various good qualities as being the necessary preliminaries to it. Human perfection resides in this, that the love of God should conquer a man's heart and possess it wholly, and even if it does not possess it wholly it should predominate in the heart over the love of all other things. Nevertheless, rightly to understand the love of God is so difficult a matter that one sect of theologians have altogether denied that man can love a Being who is not of his own species, and they have defined the love of God as consisting merely in obedience. Those who hold such views do not know what real religion is.

All Moslems are agreed that the love of God is a duty. God says concerning the believers, "He loves them and they love Him," [1] and the Prophet

[1] Koran.

said, "Till a man loves God and His Prophet more than anything else he has not the right faith." When the angel of death came to take the soul of Abraham the latter said, "Have you ever seen a friend take his friend's life?" God answered him, "Have you ever seen a friend unwilling to see his friend?" Then Abraham said, "O Azrael! take my soul!" The following prayer was taught by the Prophet to his companions, "O God, grant me to love Thee and to love those who love Thee, and whatsoever brings me nearer to Thy love, and make Thy love more precious to me than cold water to the thirsty." Hassan Basri used to say, "He who knows God loves Him, and he who knows the world hates it."

We come now to treat of love in its essential nature. Love may be defined as an inclination to that which is pleasant. This is apparent in the case of the five senses, each of which may be said to love that which gives it delight; thus the eye loves beautiful forms, the ear music, etc. This is a kind of love we share with the animals. But there is a sixth sense, or faculty of perception, implanted in the heart, which animals do not possess, through which we become aware of spiritual beauty and excellence. Thus, a man who is only acquainted with sensuous delights cannot understand what the Prophet meant when he said he loved prayer more than perfumes or women, though the last two were also pleasant to him. But he whose inner eye is opened to behold the beauty and perfection of God will despise all outward sights in comparison, however fair they may be.

The former kind of man will say that beauty resides in red-and-white complexions, well-proportioned limbs, and so forth, but he will be blind to moral beauty, such as men refer to when they speak of such and such a man as possessing a "beautiful" character. But those possessed of inner perception find it quite possible to love the departed great, such as the Caliphs Omar and Abu Bakr, on account of their noble qualities, though their bodies have long been mingled with the dust. Such love is directed not towards any outward form, but towards the inner character. Even when we wish to excite love in a child towards any one, we do not describe their outward beauty of form, etc., but their inner excellencies.

When we apply this principle to the love of God we shall find that He alone is really worthy of our love, and that, if any one loves Him not, it is because he does not know Him. Whatever we love in any one we love because it is a reflection of Him. It is for this reason that we love Muhammad, because he is the Prophet and the Beloved of God, and the love of learned and pious men is really the love of God. We shall see this more clearly if we consider what are the causes which excite love.

The first cause is this, that man loves himself and the perfection of his own nature. This leads him directly to the love of God, for man's very existence and man's attributes are nothing else but the gift of God, but for whose grace and kindness man would never have emerged from behind the curtain of non-existence into the visible world. Man's preservation and eventual attainment to perfection are also entirely dependent upon the grace of God. It would indeed be a wonder, if one should take refuge from the heat of the sun under the shadow of a tree and not be grateful to the tree, without which there would be no shadow at all. Precisely in the same way, were it not for God, man would have no existence nor attributes at all; wherefore, then, should he not love God, unless he be ignorant of Him? Doubtless fools cannot love Him, for the love of Him springs directly from the knowledge of Him, and whence should a fool have knowledge?

The second cause of this love is that man loves his benefactor, and in truth his only Benefactor is God, for whatever kindness he receives from any fellow-creature is due to the immediate instigation of God. Whatever motive may have prompted the kindness he receives from another, whether the desire to gain religious merit or a good name, God is the Agent who set that motive to work.

The third cause is the love that is aroused by

contemplation of the attributes of God, His power and wisdom, of which human power and wisdom are but the feeblest reflections. This love is akin to that we feel to the great and good men of the past, such as the Imam Malik and the Imam Shafi,[1] though we never expect to receive any personal benefits from them, and is therefore a more disinterested kind of love. God said to the prophet David, "That servant is dearest to Me who does not seek Me from fear of punishment or hope of reward, but to pay the debt due to My Deity." And in the Psalms it is written, "Who is a greater transgressor than he who worships Me from fear of hell or hope of heaven? If I had created neither, should I not then have deserved to be worshipped?"

The fourth cause of this love is the affinity between man and God, which is referred to in the saying of the Prophet, "Verily God created man in His own likeness." Furthermore, God has said, "My servant seeks proximity to Me, that I may make him My friend, and when I have made him My friend I become his ear, his eye, his tongue." Again, God said to Moses, "I was sick, and thou didst not visit Me?" Moses replied, "O God! Thou art Lord of heaven and earth: how couldest Thou be sick?" God said, "A certain servant of Mine was sick; hadst thou visited him, thou wouldst have visited Me."

[1] Founders of the sects which bear their names.

This is a somewhat dangerous topic to dwell upon, as it is beyond the understanding of common people, and even intelligent men have stumbled in treating of it, and come to believe in incarnation and union with God. Still, the affinity which does exist between man and God disposes of the objection of those theologians mentioned above, who maintain that man cannot love a Being who is not of his own species. However great the distance between them, man can love God because of the affinity indicated in the saying, "God created man in His own likeness."

The Vision of God

All Moslems profess to believe that the Vision of God is the summit of human felicity, because it is so stated in the Law; but with many this is a mere lip-profession which arouses no emotion in their hearts. This is quite natural, for how can a man long for a thing of which he has no knowledge? We will endeavour to show briefly why the Vision of God is the greatest happiness to which a man can attain.

In the first place, every one of man's faculties has its appropriate function which it delights to fulfil. This holds good of them all, from the lowest bodily appetite to the highest form of intellectual apprehension. But even a comparatively low form of mental exertion affords greater pleasure than the satisfaction of bodily appetites. Thus, if a man happens to be absorbed in a game of chess, he will not come to his meal, though repeatedly summoned. And the higher the subject-matter of our knowledge, the greater is our delight in it; for instance, we would take more pleasure in knowing the secrets of a king than the secrets of a vizier. Seeing, then, that God is the highest possible object of knowledge, the knowledge of Him must afford more delight than any other. He who knows God, even in this world, dwells, as it were, in a paradise, "the breadth of which is as the breadth of the heavens and the earth,"[1] a paradise the fruits of which no envy can prevent him plucking, and the extent of which is not narrowed by the multitude of those who occupy it.

But the delight of knowledge still falls short of the delight of vision, just as our pleasure in thinking of those we love is much less than the pleasure afforded by the actual sight of them. Our imprisonment in bodies of clay and water, and entanglement in the things of sense constitute a veil which hides the Vision of God from us, although it does not prevent our attaining to some knowledge of Him. For this reason God said to Moses on Mount Sinai, "Thou shalt not see Me."[2]

The truth of the matter is this, that, just as the

[1] Koran. [2] *Ibid.*

seed of man becomes a man, and a buried date-stone becomes a palm-tree, so the knowledge of God acquired on earth will in the next world change into the Vision of God, and he who has never learnt the knowledge will never have the Vision. This Vision will not be shared alike by all who know, but their discernment of it will vary exactly as their knowledge. God is one, but He will be seen in many different ways, just as one object is reflected in different ways by different mirrors, some showing it straight, and some distorted, some clearly and some dimly. A mirror may be so crooked as to make even a beautiful form appear misshapen, and a man may carry into the next world a heart so dark and distorted that the sight which will be a source of peace and joy to others will be to him a source of misery. He, in whose heart the love of God has prevailed over all else, will derive more joy from this vision than he in whose heart it has not so prevailed; just as in the case of two men with equally powerful eyesight, gazing on a beautiful face, he who already loves the possessor of that face will rejoice in beholding it more than he who does not. For perfect happiness mere knowledge is not enough, unaccompanied by love, and the love of God cannot take possession of a man's heart till it be purified from love of the world, which purification can only be effected by abstinence and austerity.

While he is in this world a man's condition with regard to the Vision of God is like that of a lover who should see his Beloved's face in the twilight, while his clothes are infested with hornets and scorpions, which continually torment him. But should the sun arise and reveal his Beloved's face in all its beauty, and the noxious vermin leave off molesting him, then the lover's joy will be like that of God's servant, who, released from the twilight and the tormenting trials of this world, beholds Him without a veil. Abu Suleiman said, "He who is busy with himself now will be busy with himself then, and he who is occupied with God now will be occupied with Him then."

Yahya Ibn Muaz relates, "I watched Bayazid Bistami at prayer through one entire night. When he had finished he stood up and said, 'O Lord! some of Thy servants have asked and obtained of Thee the power to perform miracles, to walk on the sea, and to fly in the air, but this I do not ask; some have asked and obtained treasures, but these I do not ask.' Then he turned, and, seeing me, said, 'Are you there, Yahya?' I replied, 'Yes.' He asked, 'Since when?' I answered, 'For a long time.' I then asked him to reveal to me some of his spiritual experiences. 'I will reveal,' he answered, 'what is lawful to tell you. The Almighty showed me His kingdom, from its loftiest to its lowest; He raised me above the throne and the seat and all the seven heavens. Then He said, "Ask of me whatsoever thing thou desirest." I answered, "Lord! I wish for nothing beside Thee." "Verily," He said, "thou art My servant."'"

On another occasion Bayazid said, "Were God to offer thee the intimacy with Himself of Abraham, the power in prayer of Moses, the spirituality of Jesus, yet keep thy face directed to Him only, for He has treasures surpassing even these." One day a friend said to him, "For thirty years I have fasted by day and prayed by night and have found none of that spiritual joy of which thou speakest." Bayazid answered, "If you fasted and prayed for three hundred years, you would never find it." "How is that?" asked the other. "Because," said Bayazid, "your selfishness is acting as a veil between you and God." "Tell me, then, the cure." "It is a cure which you cannot carry out." However, as his friend pressed him to reveal it, Bayazid said, "Go to the nearest barber and have your beard shaved; strip yourself of your clothes, with the exception of a girdle round your loins. Take a horse's nose-bag full of walnuts, hang it round your neck, go into the bazaar and cry out, 'Any boy who gives me a slap on the nape of my neck shall have a walnut.' Then, in this manner, go where the Cadi and the doctors of the law are sitting." "Bless my soul!" said his friend,

"I really can't do that; do suggest some other remedy." "This is the indispensable preliminary to a cure," answered Bayazid, "but, as I told you, you are incurable."

The reason Bayazid indicated this method of cure for want of relish in devotion was that his friend was an ambitious seeker after place and honour. Ambition and pride are diseases which can only be cured in some such way. God said unto Jesus, "O Jesus! when I see in My servants' hearts pure love for Myself unmixed with any selfish desire concerning this world or the next, I act as guardian over that love." Again, when people asked Jesus "What is the highest work of all?" he answered, "To love God and to be resigned to His will." The saint Rabia was once asked whether she loved the Prophet: "The love of the Creator," she said, "has prevented my loving the creature." Ibrahim Ben Adham, in his prayers, said, "O God! In my eyes heaven itself is less than a gnat in comparison with the love of Thee and the joy of Thy remembrance which Thou hast granted me."

He who supposes that it is possible to enjoy happiness in the next world apart from the love of God is far gone in error, for the very essence of the future life is to arrive at God as at an Object of desire long aimed at and attained through countless obstacles. This enjoyment of God is happiness. But if he had no delight in

God before, he will not delight in Him then, and if his joy in God was but slight before it will be but slight then. In brief, our future happiness will be in strict proportion to the degree in which we have loved God here.

But (and may God preserve us from such a doom !) if in a man's heart there has been growing up a love of what is opposed to God, the conditions of the next life will be altogether alien to him, and that which will cause joy to others will to him cause misery.

This may be illustrated by the following anecdote: A certain scavenger went into the perfume-sellers' bazaar, and, smelling the sweet scents, fell down unconscious. People came round him and sprinkled rose-water upon him and held musk to his nose, but he only became worse. At last one came who had been a scavenger himself; he held a little filth under the man's nose and he revived instantly, exclaiming, with a sigh of satisfaction, "Ah! this is perfume indeed!" Thus in the next life a worldling will no longer find the filthy lucre and the filthy pleasures of the world; the spiritual joys of that world will be altogether alien to him and but increase his wretchedness. For the next world is a world of Spirit and of the manifestation of the Beauty of God; happy is that man who has aimed at and acquired affinity with it. All austerities, devotions, studies have the acquirement of that affinity for their aim, and that affinity is love. This is the meaning of that saying of the Koran, "He who has purified his soul is happy." Sins and lusts directly oppose the attainment of this affinity; therefore the Koran goes on to say, "And he who has corrupted his soul is miserable."[1] Those who are gifted with spiritual insight have really grasped this truth as a fact of experience, and not a merely traditional maxim. Their clear perception of it leads them to the conviction that he by whom it was spoken was a prophet indeed, just as a man who has studied medicine knows when he is listening to a physician. This is a kind of certainty which requires no support from miracles such as the conversion of a rod into a snake, the credit of which may be shaken by apparently equally extraordinary miracles performed by magicians.

The Signs of the Love of God

Many claim to love God, but each should examine himself as to the genuineness of the love which he professes. The first test is this: he should not dislike the thought of death, for no friend shrinks from going to see a friend. The Prophet said, "Whoever wishes to see God, God wishes to see him." It is true a sincere lover of

[1] Koran, chap. 91.

God may shrink from the thought of death coming before he has finished his preparation for the next world, but if he *is* sincere, he will be diligent in making such preparation.

The second test of sincerity is that a man should be willing to sacrifice his will to God's, should cleave to what brings him nearer to God, and should shun what places him at a distance from God. The fact of a man's sinning is no proof that he does not love God at all, but it proves that he does not love Him with his whole heart. The saint Fudhail said to a certain man, "If any one asks you whether you love God, keep silent; for if you say, 'I do not love Him,' you are an infidel; and if you say, 'I do,' your deeds contradict you."

The third test is that the remembrance of God should always remain fresh in a man's heart without effort, for what a man loves he constantly remembers, and if his love is perfect he never forgets it. It is possible, however, that, while the love of God does not take the first place in a man's heart, the love of the love of God may, for love is one thing and the love of love another.

The fourth test is, that he will love the Koran, which is the Word of God, and Muhammad, who is the Prophet of God; if his love is really strong, he will love all men, for all are God's servants, nay, his love will embrace the whole creation, for he who loves any one loves the works he composes and his handwriting.

The fifth test is, he will be covetous of retirement and privacy for purposes of devotion; he will long for the approach of night, so that he may hold intercourse with his Friend without let or hindrance. If he prefers conversation by day and sleep at night to such retirement, then his love is imperfect. God said to David, "Be not too intimate with men; for two kinds of persons are excluded from My presence: those who are earnest in seeking reward and slack when they obtain it, and those who prefer their own thoughts to the remembrance of Me. The sign of My displeasure is, that I leave such to themselves."

In truth, if the love of God really take possession of the heart all other love is excluded. One of the children of Israel was in the habit of praying at night, but, observing that a bird sang in a certain tree very sweetly, he began to pray under that tree, in order to have the pleasure of listening to the bird. God told David to go and say to him, "Thou hast mingled the love of a melodious bird with the love of Me; thy rank among the saints is lowered." On the other hand, some have loved God with such intensity that, while they were engaged in devotion, their houses have caught fire and they have not noticed it.

A sixth test is that worship becomes easy. A

certain saint said, "During one space of thirty years I performed my night-devotions with great difficulty, but during a second space of thirty years they became a delight." When love to God is complete no joy is equal to the joy of worship.

The seventh test is that lovers of God will love those who obey Him and hate the infidels and the disobedient, as the Koran says: "They are strenuous against the unbelievers and merciful to each other." The Prophet once asked God and said, "O Lord! who are Thy lovers?" and the answer came, "Those who cleave to Me as a child to its mother, take refuge in the remembrance of Me as a bird seeks the shelter of its nest, and are as angry at the sight of sin as an angry lion who fears nothing."

Printed by Hazell, Watson & Viney, Ld., London and Aylesbury.

THE WISDOM OF THE EAST SERIES

Edited by L. CRANMER-BYNG and Dr. S. A. KAPADIA

THE SERIES AND ITS PURPOSE

THE object of the Editors of this Series is a very definite one. They desire above all things that, in their humble way, these books shall be the ambassadors of good-will and understanding between East and West—the old world of Thought and the new of Action. In this endeavour, and in their own sphere, they are but followers of the highest example in the land. They are confident that a deeper knowledge of the great ideals and lofty philosophy of Oriental thought may help to a revival of that true spirit of Charity which neither despises nor fears the nations of another creed and colour. Finally, in thanking press and public for the very cordial reception given to the "Wisdom of the East" Series, they wish to state that no pains have been spared to secure the best specialists for the treatment of the various subjects at hand.

NEW VOLUMES

In the Press

THE RUBAIYÁT OF HAFIZ. Translated with Introduction. by SYED ABDUL MAJID, LL.D. Rendered into English Verse by L. CRANMER-BYNG. 1/- net.

A CHINESE QUIETIST. From the Mystical Philosophy of Liehtze. Translated by LIONEL GILES, M.A. 2/- net.

THE BUSTAN OF SA'DI. From the Persian. Translated with Introduction by A. HART EDWARDS. 2/- net.

[*Continued over*

Just Out

THE ALCHEMY OF HAPPINESS. By AL GHAZZALI. Rendered into English by CLAUD FIELD 2/- net.

THE SINGING CARAVAN. Some Echoes of Arabian Poetry. By HENRY BAERLEIN. 2/- net.

THE WISDOM OF THE APOCRYPHA. With an Introduction by C. E. LAWRENCE, Author of "Pilgrimage," etc. 2/- net.

THE BURDEN OF ISIS. Being the Laments of Isis and Nephthys. Translated from the Egyptian with an Introduction by JAMES TEACKLE DENNIS. 1/- net.

THE MASTER-SINGERS OF JAPAN. Being Verse Translations from the Japanese Poets. By CLARA A. WALSH. 2/- net.

THE PATH OF LIGHT. Rendered for the first time into English from the Bodhi-charyāvatāra of Śānti-Deva. A Manual of Mahā-Yāna Buddhism. By L. D. Barnett, M.A. Litt.D. 2/- net.

THE SPLENDOUR OF GOD. Being Extracts from the Sacred Writings of the Bahais. With Introduction by ERIC HAMMOND. 2/- net.

A LUTE OF JADE. Being Selections from the Classical Poets of China. Rendered with an Introduction by L. CRANMER-BYNG. 2/- net.

THE CONFESSIONS OF AL GHAZZALI. Translated for the first time into English by CLAUD FIELD, M.A. 1/- net.

THE HEART OF INDIA. Sketches in the History of Hindu Religion and Morals. By L. D. BARNETT, M.A., LITT.D., Professor of Sanskrit at University College, London. 2/- net.

THE BOOK OF FILIAL DUTY. Translated from the Chinese of the Hsiao Ching by IVAN CHÊN, first Secretary to the Chinese Legation. 1/- net.

THE DIWAN OF ABU'L-ALA. By HENRY BAERLEIN. 1/- net.

BRAHMA-KNOWLEDGE: An Outline of the Philosophy of the Vedānta. As set forth by the Upanishads and by Sankara. By L. D. BARNETT, M.A., LITT.D., Professor of Sanskrit at University College, London. 2/- net.

THE CONDUCT OF LIFE; or, The Universal Order of Confucius. A translation of one of the four Confucian Books, hitherto known as the Doctrine of the Mean. By KU HUNG MING, M.A. (Edin.). 1/- net.

THE TEACHINGS OF ZOROASTER. Translated with Introduction by Dr. S. A. KAPADIA, Lecturer, University College, London. 2/- net.

THE PERSIAN MYSTICS.

I. Jalálu'd-dín Rúmí. By F. HADLAND DAVIS. 2/- net.

II. Jámí. By F. HADLAND DAVIS. 2/- net.

THE WAY OF THE BUDDHA. Selections from the Buddhist texts, together with the original Pali, with Introduction by HERBERT BAYNES, M.R.A.S. 2/- net.

THE SAYINGS OF CONFUCIUS. A new Translation of the greater part of the Confucian Analects, with Introduction and Notes by LIONEL GILES, M.A. (Oxon.), Assistant in the Department of Oriental Books and Manuscripts of the British Museum. 2/- net.

MUSINGS OF A CHINESE MYSTIC. Selections from the Philosophy of Chuang Tzŭ. With Introduction by LIONEL GILES, M.A. (Oxon.), Assistant at the British Museum. 2/- net.

THE AWAKENING OF THE SOUL. From the Arabic of IBN TUFAIL. Translated with Introduction by PAUL BRÖNNLE, Ph.D. 1/6 net.

THE RELIGION OF THE KORAN. With Introduction by Sir ARTHUR N. WOLLASTON, K.C.I.E. 1/- net.

THE WISDOM OF ISRAEL: Being Extracts from the Babylonian Talmud and Midrash Rabboth. Translated from the Aramaic with an Introduction by EDWIN COLLINS. 1/- net.

SA'DI'S SCROLL OF WISDOM. By SHAIKH SA'DI. With Introduction by Sir ARTHUR N. WOLLASTON, K.C.I.E. 1/- net. With Persian Script added. 2/- net.

THE INSTRUCTION OF PTAH-HOTEP AND THE INSTRUCTION OF KE'GEMNI. The Oldest Books in the World. Translated from the Egyptian with Introduction and Appendix by BATTISCOMBE G. GUNN. 1/- net.

THE ROSE GARDEN OF SA'DI. Selected and Rendered from the Persian with Introduction by L. CRANMER-BYNG. 1/- net.

THE CLASSICS OF CONFUCIUS.

I. The Book of History (Shu-King) By W. GORN OLD. 1/- net.

II. The Book of Odes (Shi-King). By L. CRANMER-BYNG. 1/- net.

THE SAYINGS OF LAO TZŬ. From the Chinese. Translated with Introduction by LIONEL GILES, of the British Museum. 1/- net.

WOMEN AND WISDOM OF JAPAN. With Introduction by S. TAKAISHI. 1/- net.

ARABIAN WISDOM. Selections and Translations from the Arabic by JOHN WORTABET, M.D. 1/- net.

THE DUTIES OF THE HEART. By RABBI BACHYE. Translated from the Hebrew with Introduction by EDWIN COLLINS, Hollier Hebrew Scholar, U.C.L. 1/- net.

ROMANCE OF THE EAST SERIES

Edited by L. CRANMER-BYNG

Crown 8vo. 2s. 6d. net each.

IN this series the great store-houses of Oriental romance will be opened for the first time to the public. Tales from the Sanskrit, from the Chinese, from every language of the East possessing a great literature will appear in due course. From these vivid narratives of old-world romance it will be possible for the reader to glean much information concerning the lives and manners and customs of vanished races, and the greatness of Empires that have passed away.

TALES OF THE CALIPHS. From the Arabic
Translated by CLAUD FIELD

TALES WITHIN TALES. From the Fables of Pilpai
Translated by Sir ARTHUR WOLLASTON, K.C.I.E.

THE GOLDEN TOWN. From the Sanskrit of Soma Deva
Translated by Dr. L. D. BARNETT.

Works added to the Series will be announced in due course

LONDON
JOHN MURRAY, ALBEMARLE STREET, W.